PENGUIN BOOKS
IN THEIR OWN VOICE

Arlene R. K. Zide was born in 1940 in New York City. She holds a Ph.D. from the University of Chicago in Linguistics and South Asian Languages. A linguist, poet and translator, her poetry has appeared in numerous journals in India and the US, for example, in *Oyez Review, City, The Colorado North Review, The Spoon River Quarterly, Cumberlands, Bloodroot, Encore, Off Our Backs, Salome, Primavera, Manushi, Debonair, Femina*, and some poems in translation in *The Observer* (Hindi edition) and *Istahar* (Oriya). Ten of her poems were recently selected for *Poet-Linguists* (Jupiter Press, Swarthmore). Her translations have appeared in the *P.E.N., Debonair, East Point* and *Pratibha* in India, and in the *Chicago Review* and *Literary Olympians 1992*, and will appear in the *Oxford Anthology of Indian Poets* and the *Malahat Review*. A book of translations of contemporary Oriya women poets, *Under A Silent Sun*, with the poet J. P. Das, was published in 1992. On a recent Fulbright scholarship to India, she collected and translated poetry for this anthology.

At present, Dr Zide is an Associate Professor, Harold Washington College (City Colleges of Chicago) in the departments of Foreign Language/ESL and Humanities, and an Associate of the Committee on Southern Asian Studies, University of Chicago. She is also a co-editor of *Primavera*, a women's literary and arts journal published from Chicago.

IN THEIR OWN VOICE

The Penguin Anthology of Contemporary Indian Women Poets

Compiled and edited with an introduction by
Dr Arlene R. K. Zide

PENGUIN BOOKS

Penguin Books India (P) Ltd., 210 Chiranjiv Towers, 43 Nehru Place, New Delhi-110019, India
Penguin Books Ltd., 27 Wrights Lane, London W8 5TZ, UK
Penguin Books USA Inc., 375 Hudson Street, New York, N.Y. 10014, USA
Penguin Books Australia Ltd., Ringwood, Victoria, Australia
Penguin Books Canada Ltd., 10 Alcorn Avenue, Suite 300, Toronto, Ontario M4V 3B2, Canada.
Penguin Books (NZ) Ltd., 182-190 Wairau Road, Auckland 10, New Zealand.

First published by Penguin Books India (P) Ltd. 1993

Copyright © Penguin Books India (P) Ltd, 1993

All rights reserved

10 9 8 7 6 5 4 3 2

Typeset in Palatino by dTech Services Pvt. Ltd., New Delhi

This book is sold subject to the condition that it shall not, by way of trade or otherwise, be lent, resold, hired out, or otherwise circulated without the publisher's prior written consent in any form of binding or cover other than that in which it is published and without a similar condition including this condition being imposed on the subsequent purchaser and without limiting the rights under copyright reserved above, no part of this publication may be reproduced, stored in or introduced into a retrieval system, or transmitted in any form or by any means (electronic, mechanical, photocopying, recording or otherwise), without the prior written permission of both the copyright owner and the above-mentioned publisher of this book.

for my sons, Bill and Greg

and
for Joan Erdman
without whose faith, encouragement and ingenuity
this volume might never have been dared

ACKNOWLEDGEMENTS

While every effort has been made to ensure that permission to reproduce copyright material included in the book was obtained, in the event of any inadvertent omission, the publishers should be notified and formal acknowledgements will be included in all future editions of this book.

The editor and publishers would like to thank the following for granting permission to use their poems in this volume :

- Shanta Acharya for 'A Giddy Mannequin';
- Indrani Aikath-Gyaltsen for 'The Widower';
- Meena Alexander for 'House of a Thousand Doors' © Meena Alexander, which was first published in *House of a Thousand Doors* (Three Continents Press, Washington DC, 1988) and 'No Man's Land' which was first published in *New Letters* (1990);
- Malika Amar Shaikh for 'Megalopolis 1' and 'Megalopolis 9';
- Bala for 'from You and You—Me and Me' and 'You and I';
- Balamani Amma for 'At the pond';
- Banaja Devi for 'On my own grave';
- Sangjukta Bandyopadhyay for 'Not a goddess';
- Shukla Bandyopadhyay for 'Holding the hand of a serial love';
- Hira Bansode for 'Woman' and 'Look, Mother';
- Nirmal Prabha Bardoloi for 'He would have come long ago' and 'I am there';
- Anjana Basu for 'Yellow' and 'No Nuclear night, Bhopal';
- Krishna Basu for 'Gold Coins';
- Ishita Bhaduri for 'Twenty-seven million years later';
- Shobha Bhagwat for 'Husbands';
- Amrita Bharati for 'The Snake and the Man';

- Sujata Bhatt for 'Udaylee' and 'White Asparagus';
- Manorama Mahapatra Biswal for 'My whole life for him';
- Bratati Biswas for 'The Temptation Which';
- Cantirakanti for 'Wanted: A Broom';
- P. Lal, Writers Workshop, Calcutta, for Margaret Chatterjee's poem 'From The Abyss' from *The Spring and the Spectacle* © Writers Workshop, Calcutta;
- Chaitali Chattopadhyay for 'Rage';
- Gita Chattopadhyay for 'The Ritual of Sati' and 'Thirty-five Parganas';
- Snehmayee Chaudhary for 'The Lucky Ones';
- Kirti Chaudhury for 'Contentment';
- Mahuya Chaudhury for 'The Tribe';
- The estate of Bahinabai Choudhury for 'Life';
- Vijaya Dabbe for 'Call them what you will';
- Aziz Bano Darab for 'The Season of Rains' and 'Ghazals';
- Bijoyini Das for 'Kubuja';
- Jyotsna Das for 'Coincidence';
- Kamala Das for 'An Introduction' and 'The Old Playhouse';
- Yashodara Das for 'Dharmapada';
- Mamata Dash for 'Murderer';
- Gauri Deshpande for 'Workaday Women' and 'The Female of the Species';
- Eunice de Souza for 'Poem for a poet', and 'Idyll' and 'Transcend Self You Say';
- Nabaneeta Dev Sen for 'The Child's Saying' and 'Sometimes, Love';
- Oxford University Press, New Delhi, for Imtiaz Dharker's poems 'Purdah I' and 'Grace' from *Purdah*;
- Aruna Dhere for 'Night has come to an end';
- Ashwini Dhongde for 'Small Ads';
- Saroop Dhruv for 'Princess Desire' and 'I Ask—"Why?"';
- Chitra Divakaruni for 'Making samosas' and 'The Brides come to Yuba City';
- Orient Longman Limited, Hyderabad for Charmayne D'Souza's poem 'Miss-Begotten';
- Ketaki Kushari Dyson for 'After Reading Nawal El Saadawi's Book—*The Hidden Face of Eve*';
- Pia Ganguli for 'Choices of a King's Mistress' and 'About the Lady who buys a pint of Vodka 'twice a day';

- Prabha Ganorkar for 'Language';
- Gagan Gill for 'She will come back in her body' and 'The Fifth Man';
- Padma Gole for 'The Dread of Motherhood' and 'There's still something left';
- Teji Grover for 'Song of separation';
- Kamala Hemmige for 'Do you know?';
- Popati Hiranandani for 'A rare treasure';
- Ivara (V. Indira Bhavani) for 'Avatars';
- Sunita Jain for 'What is it';
- Nayana Jani for 'The Soundless Explosion';
- Jaya Prabha for 'Looks';
- Bhagya Jayasudarshana for 'For Akka';
- Mamta Kalia for 'Marital Bliss';
- M. R. Kamala for 'Dreams on sale';
- Lakshmi Kannan for 'Draupadi';
- Manju Kapur for 'Birds';
- Ketu Katrak for 'Memories of Exile';
- Katyayani for 'Champa, among seven brothers' and 'The lump of jaggery';
- Krishnakumari for 'Carbon Dioxide';
- Kamal Kumar for 'New Generation';
- Kusum for 'from I wanted to have a daughter';
- Apabrita Lahiri for 'Firstness' and 'Permission';
- Chitra Lahiri for 'Ravaged Blossom';
- Jyoti Lanjewar for 'I never saw you';
- Joyshree Lobo for 'The Jackals wait below';
- Pravasini Mahakud for 'Before anyone comes';
- Anuradha Mahapatra for 'God' and 'Businesswoman's Story';
- Uma Maheswari for 'Of My Own';
- Sujatha Mathai for 'Ishvari's Voice' which was first published in a special issue on Indian writing in *Chelsea*, New York;
- Shakunt Mathur for 'Chilka Lake' and 'Waiting';
- R. Meenakshi for 'I'll Sing For Mankind—O Ad Man'; and 'O Heroine of Madurai';
- Jaya Mehta for 'A Further Question' and an untitled poem;
- Memchoubi (Arambam Ongbi Ibemhal) for 'The Goddess Of Lightning';
- Jyotsna Milan for 'Wind-tree' and 'Woman - 2';
- Sanghamitra Mishra for 'Sorrow';

- Sucheta Mishra for 'Distance';
- Yashodhara Mishra for 'The Sea';
- Debarati Mitra for 'Paloma College';
- Aparna Mohanty for her untitled poem;
- Brahmotri Mohanty for 'Faith';
- Giribala Mohanty for 'Good News Bad News';
- Nirmala Mohanty for 'The Peddlar';
- Sasmita Mohanty for 'Mistress' and 'Wife';
- Kanchankuntala Mukherjee for 'Along the railroad track';
- Vijaya Mukhopadhyay for 'Companion' and 'Advertisement';
- Mukthayakka for 'Little Poems';
- Vrinda Nabar for 'Oxford Ode';
- Lalitha Naik for 'Small Change';
- Panna Naik for 'Seed' and 'Talk';
- Pratibha Nandakumar for 'Poem';
- Tejaswini Niranjana for 'Pictures—Poems for unredeemed kinship';
- Kondepudi Nirmala for 'Labour Room';
- Jameela Nishat for her four untitled poems;
- Mrinal Pande for 'Two Women Knitting' and 'Her Home';
- Uma Parameswaran for 'I wish I knew what to tell you, My Daughters';
- Geeta Parikh for 'There is joy';
- Rajani Parulekar for 'The Snake Couple' and 'A torrent of people and words';
- Anuradha Patil for 'Square-Knot';
- Hema Pattanshetti for 'A Voice';
- Anuradha Potdar for 'Motherhood';
- Amrita Pritam for 'Virgin' and 'Creative Process';
- Savitri Rajeevan for 'The Day' and 'A pair of glasses';
- Rajlukshmee Debee for 'Cophetua';
- Nita Pramod Ramaiya for 'The year of 1979' and 'A young woman's resolution to protect herself';
- Anuradha Ramanan for 'The Verdict';
- C. Vimala Rao for 'A Scene';
- Pratima Ray for 'Harvest Moon';
- Vaddera Chandidas for Revathi Devi's 'This Night', 'Silalolita (Stone Tossed)' and 'The Voice';
- Anuradha Marwah Roy for her untitled poem;

- Padma Sachdev for 'Long Hair' and 'These King's Palaces, Are They Yours';
- Malavika Rajbans Sanghvi for 'Growing Old';
- Indira Sant for 'Alone';
- Sarvamangala for 'Doll';
- Yashodhara Sathe for her untitled poem;
- Pratibha Satpathy for 'Insect' and 'The Falklands';
- K. Aparna for Savithri's 'Dacoits';
- Nilima Sen-Gangopadhyay for 'Fission';
- Mallika Sengupta for 'The Carriers of Fire', 'Robot' and 'Home';
- Rajee Seth for 'Bungalow on the mountain' and 'My Sisters';
- Rita Shahani for 'And the knitting goes on';
- Shafiq Fatima Sheira for 'The city of the voice' and 'The play of the seasons (Ellora)';
- Shanta Shelke for 'On my way back' and 'If you look at it like that';
- Shree Devi for 'On a shikar' and 'Last night at 3 a.m.';
- Beheroze F. Shroff for 'Mother' and 'Bridge and tea party';
- Melanie Silgardo for 'Doris';
- Ila Rani Singh for 'Misfit';
- Kabita Sinha for 'Curse' and 'Eve speaks to God';
- Sugathakumari for 'The rain at night';
- Sukrita for 'A borrowed existence';
- Thilakavathi for 'Woman, this, too, is a wound to be proud of';
- Manjit Tiwana for 'Husband';
- Sunanda Tripathy for 'The Tryst' and 'Poem in motion';
- S. Usha for 'To Mother';
- Vaidehi (Janaki Srinivasmurthy) for 'Girl in the kitchen'';
- Archana Verma for 'Man' and 'Kite';
- Shefalika Verma for 'My Village';
- Vimala for 'Kitchen';

The editor and publishers would like to thank the following for granting permission to use their translations in this volume:

- Paramita Banerjee;
- Sujata Bhatt;
- Chandrika Balan;

- Enakshi Chatterjee;
- J. P. Das;
- Tilottama Daswani;
- Jyotirmoy Datta;
- Gauri Deshpande;
- Vinay Dharwadker;
- Chitra Divakaruni;
- Hiren Gohain;
- Hrydayakumari;
- Qurratulain Hyder;
- Lakshmi Kannan;
- Ashok Kelkar;
- Arun Kolatkar;
- Jayanta Mahapatra;
- Asha Mundlay;
- Panna Naik;
- Tejaswini Niranjana;
- Mrinal Pande;
- Ayyappa Paniker;
- Mrs. P. Shenbagavally for K. Paramasivam's translations;
- Bharat Pathak;
- A. K. Ramanujan;
- Velcheru Narayana Rao;
- C. Rama Rao;
- V. V. B. Rama Rao;
- Sunil B. Ray;
- Sandhya S.;
- Sulekha Samantaray;
- Martha Ann Selby;
- Arabinda Nath Sharma;
- Ramachandra Sharma;
- L. Joychandra Singh;
- Anjani K. Sinha;
- Syed Sirajuddin;
- Aruna Sitesh;
- Emdad Ullah;
- Carolyne Wright;

CONTENTS

Acknowledgements — vii
Introduction by Arlene Zide — xix

SHANTA ACHARYA: *A Giddy Mannequin* — 1
INDRANI AIKATH-GYALTSEN: *The Widower* — 2
MEENA ALEXANDER: *House of a thousand doors* — 3
    No Man's Land — 4
MALIKA AMAR SHAIKH: *Megalopolis 1* — 5
    Megalopolis 9 — 6
BALA: *From You and You—Me and Me* — 8
    You and I — 8
BALAMANI AMMA: *At the pond* — 9
BANAJA DEVI: *On my own grave* — 12
SANGJUKTA BANDYOPADHYAY: *Not a goddess* — 13
SHUKLA BANDYOPADHYAY: *Holding the hand of a serial love* — 14
HIRA BANSODE: *Woman* — 15
    Look, Mother — 15
NIRMAL PRABHA BARDOLOI: *He would have come long ago* — 17
    I am there — 18
    Untitled — 18
ANJANA BASU: *Yellow* — 19
    No Nuclear night, Bhopal — 19
KRISHNA BASU: *Gold Coins* — 20
ISHITA BHADURI: *Twenty-seven million years later* — 21
SHOBHA BHAGWAT: *Husbands* — 22
AMRITA BHARATI: *The Snake and the Man* — 23
SUJATA BHATT: *Udaylee* — 24
    White Asparagus — 24

MANORAMA MAHAPATRA BISWAL: *My whole life for Him*	26
BRATATI BISWAS: *The Temptation Which*	27
CANTIRAKANTI: *Wanted: A Broom*	28
MARGARET CHATTERJEE: *From the Abyss*	29
CHAITALI CHATTOPADHYAY: *Rage*	31
GITA CHATTOPADHYAY: *The Ritual of Sati*	32
Thirty-five Parganas	33
SNEHMAYEE CHAUDHARY: *The Lucky Ones*	34
KIRTI CHAUDHURY: *Contentment*	35
MAHUYA CHAUDHURY: *The Tribe*	36
BAHINABAI CHOUDHURY: *Life*	37
VIJAYA DABBE: *Call them what you will*	38
AZIZ BANO DARAB: *The Season of Rains*	40
Ghazals	41
BIJOYINI DAS: *Kubuja*	42
JYOTSNA DAS: *Coincidence*	44
KAMALA DAS: *An Introduction*	45
The Old Playhouse	46
YASHODARA DAS: *Dharmapada*	48
MAMATA DASH: *Murderer*	50
GAURI DESHPANDE: *Workaday Women*	52
The Female of the Species	53
EUNICE DE SOUZA: *Poem for a poet*	54
Idyll	55
NABANEETA DEV SEN: *The Child's Saying*	56
Sometimes, Love	56
IMTIAZ DHARKER: *Purdah I*	58
Grace	59
ARUNA DHERE: *Night has come to an end*	61
ASHWINI DHONGDE: *Small Ads*	62
SAROOP DHRUV: *Princess Desire*	63
I Ask - 'Why?'	65
CHITRA BANERJEE DIVAKARUNI: *Making samosas*	68
The Brides come to Yuba City	69
CHARMAYNE D'SOUZA: *Miss-Begotten*	71
KETAKI KUSHARI DYSON: *After reading Nawal El Saadawi's Book—The Hidden Face of Eve*	72

PIA GANGULI: *Choices of a King's Mistress*	74
About the Lady who buys a pint of Vodka twice a day	74
PRABHA GANORKAR: *Language*	75
GAGAN GILL: *She will come back in her body*	77
The Fifth Man	78
PADMA GOLE: *The Dread of Motherhood*	79
There's still something left	80
TEJI GROVER: *Song of separation*	81
KAMALA HEMMIGE: *Do you know?*	83
POPATI HIRANANDANI: *A rare treasure*	84
IVARA (V. INDIRA BHAVANI): *Avatars*	85
SUNITA JAIN: *What is it*	88
NAYANA JANI: *The Soundless Explosion*	90
JAYA PRABHA: *Looks*	91
BHAGYA JAYASUDARSHANA: *For Akka*	93
MAMTA KALIA: *Marital Bliss*	94
M. R. KAMALA: *Dreams on sale*	95
LAKSHMI KANNAN: *Draupadi*	97
MANJU KAPUR: *Birds*	99
KETU KATRAK: *Memories of Exile*	100
KATYAYANI: *Champa, among seven brothers*	102
The lump of jaggery	103
N. KRISHNA KUMARI: *Carbon Dioxide*	105
KAMAL KUMAR: *New Generation*	107
KUSUM: *from I wanted to have a daughter*	108
APABRITA LAHIRI: *Firstness*	110
Permission	110
CHITRA LAHIRI: *Ravaged Blossom*	111
JYOTI LANJEWAR: *I never saw you*	112
JOYSHREE LOBO: *The Jackals wait below*	116
PRAVASINI MAHAKUD: *Before anyone comes*	118
ANURADHA MAHAPATRA: *God*	121
Businesswoman's Story	122
UMA MAHESWARI: *Of My Own*	123
SUJATHA MATHAI: *Ishvari's Voice*	124
SHAKUNT MATHUR: *Chilka Lake*	125
Waiting	126
R. MEENAKSHI: *I'll Sing For Mankind—O Ad Man*	127
O Heroine of Madurai	128

JAYA MEHTA: *A Further Question*	129
Untitled	129
MEMCHOUBI (Arambam Ongbi Ibemhal): *The Goddess of Lighting*	130
JYOTSNA MILAN: *Wind-tree*	131
Woman - 2	132
SANGHAMITRA MISHRA: *Sorrow*	133
SUCHETA MISHRA: *Distance*	135
YASHODHARA MISHRA: *The Sea*	136
DEBARATI MITRA: *Paloma College*	137
APARNA MOHANTY: Untitled	138
BRAHMOTRI MOHANTY: *Faith*	141
GIRIBALA MOHANTY: *Good News Bad News*	142
NIRMALA MOHANTY: *The Pedlar*	143
SASMITA MOHANTY: *Mistress*	145
Wife	145
KANCHANKUNTALA MUKHERJEE: *Along the railroad track*	147
VIJAYA MUKHOPADHYAY: *Companion*	149
Advertisement	149
MUKTHAYAKKA: *Little Poems*	150
VRINDA NABAR: *Oxford Ode*	152
LALITHA NAIK: *Small Change*	154
PANNA NAIK: *Seed*	155
Talk	156
PRATIBHA NANDAKUMAR: *Poem*	157
TEJASWINI NIRANJANA: *Pictures—Poems for unredeemed kinship*	159
KONDEPUDI NIRMALA: *Labour Room*	164
JAMEELA NISHAT: Untitled	166
Untitled	166
Untitled	167
Untitled	167
MRINAL PANDE: *Two Women Knitting*	169
Her Home	170
UMA PARAMESWARAN: *I wish I knew what to tell you, my daughters*	171
GEETA PARIKH: *There is joy*	174
RAJANI PARULEKAR: *The Snake Couple*	176
A torrent of people and words	176
ANURADHA PATIL: *Square-knot*	178
HEMA PATTANSHETTI: *A Voice*	179

ANURADHA POTDAR: *Motherhood*	180
AMRITA PRITAM: *Virgin*	181
Creative Process	181
SAVITRI RAJEEVAN: *The Day*	183
A pair of glasses	184
RAJLUKSHMEE DEBEE: *Cophetua*	186
NITA PRAMOD RAMAIYA: *The year of 1979*	187
A young woman's resolution to protect herself	188
ANURADHA RAMANAN: *The Verdict*	190
C. VIMALA RAO: *A Scene*	191
PRATIMA RAY: *Harvest Moon*	192
REVATHI DEVI: *This Night*	193
Silalolita (Stone Tossed)	194
The Voice	195
ANURADHA MARWAH ROY: *Untitled*	196
PADMA SACHDEV: *Long hair*	197
These king's places, are they yours	198
MALAVIKA RAJBANS SANGHVI: *Growing Old*	200
INDIRA SANT: *Alone*	201
SARVAMANGALA: *Doll*	202
YASHODHARA SATHE: *Untitled*	204
PRATIBHA SATPATHY: *Insect*	205
The Falklands	206
SAVITHRI: *Dacoits*	208
NILIMA SEN-GANGOPADHYAY: *Fission*	209
MALLIKA SENGUPTA: *The carriers of fire*	210
Home	210
Robot	211
RAJEE SETH: *Bungalow on the mountain*	212
My Sisters	213
RITA SHAHANI: *And the knitting goes on*	214
SHAKUNTALA DEVI: *Magician*	215
SHAFIQ FATIMA SHEIRA: *The city of the voice*	216
The play of the seasons (Ellora)	218
SHANTA SHELKE: *On my way back*	220
If you look at it like that	220
SHREE DEVI: *On a shikar*	221
Last night at 3 a.m.	222
BEHEROZE F. SHROFF: *Mother*	223
Bridge and tea party	224

MELANIE SILGARDO: *Doris*	225
ILA RANI SINGH: *Misfit*	226
KABITA SINHA: *Curse*	227
Eve speaks to God	227
SUGATHAKUMARI: *The rain at night*	230
SUKRITA: *A borrowed existence*	232
THILAKAVATHI: *Woman, this, too, is a wound to be proud of*	233
MANJIT TIWANA: *Husband*	236
SUNANDA TRIPATHY: *The Tryst*	237
Poem in motion	238
SA. USHA: *To Mother*	239
VAIDEHI (JANAKI SRINIVASMURTHY): *Girl in the kitchen*	240
ARCHANA VERMA: *Man*	242
Kite	243
SHEFALIKA VERMA: *My Village*	244
VIMALA: *Kitchen*	245
Notes on Authors and Translators	249

INTRODUCTION

'Transcend! Become "universal"! When will you stop writing as a woman?'

Hindi poet Gagan Gill asks, 'If I am born with that sex can I write as something other than what I am? Are men "universal"?'

Her words are personal, her own; but she reflects the views of most of the women poets in this anthology.[1] Beheroze Shroff's words too reflect this view: 'We need to stop seeing each other through men's eyes (and language!); we have to have a different "women's voice"....' Hence the title of this volume: *'In Their Own Voice'*, not **Her** individual voice, or a cacophony of their separate, individual **Voices**, but focusing on seeing through women's eyes, a different women's-eyed view of the world in poetry—their own collective women's 'voice'.

Eunice de Souza says:

> What I am as a poet is a result of what I am in all the aspects of my life. I am different from other Indian women in my form of expression; what is individual is that I am willing to take the risk. But women's experience and socialization as a whole is different. So it is expected that what they write will be different. The point is not to *not* have these differences but to be aware of them. Though all poets take risks, only women can really talk about their lives. The battle is to validate the material to begin with—the stuff of women's lives, women's experience, not to 'transcend' being a woman. The whole level of discussion is different for male and female poets—when women talk about their lives, it's 'confession', but when men do....

TRANSCEND SELF YOU SAY

Transcend self, you say
Connect with myth, history,
the world crumbling around you.
Men can, and do. Beggars survive
Destitutes survive. There's something in this culture.

Must ask beggars how they do it.

Smart arse. Poetess.

Friend, the histories I know aren't fit to print.
Remember Padma, widowed at seventeen,
Forbidden to see the sun for a year,
allowed out to crap only at night
when the pure were out of the way?

The perfect book is
one long cry in the dark.
A novelist said that
who spent his life wondering why,
when the Nazis came,
his mother pushed *him* into a closet,
and let his sisters go to Auschwitz.

Nabaneeta Dev Sen, too, is most vocal on the question of the validity of what women have to say, 'There has been a silencing of women, simply by not reading what women write. When they want to praise you they say, "you write like a man". I don't like this; "like a man" means reaching towards a certain standard—a male standard which makes women less honest.'

Her poetry is a reflection of personal responses to various situations, inside or outside, relationships with people. When asked her reaction to the fact that women are often criticized for being personal, for being 'subjective', she replied that even political poems are personal!

> What is wrong with poems which are subjective, or emotional, so long as they are well-crafted, transformed into art? Why write things which should be in an article form as a poem. After all, what is prose for? Some experiences demand a poem and others demand prose. The pain chooses its form.
>
> I challenge the validity of the questioning of the validity of women's experience. Why question the validity of emotion—that is the grammar of poetry. Emotion and reason co-exist in real life and fulfil two different purposes, both very important, but both equally valid. Why is it that when a soldier dies (and a man writes about it) that is 'universal', but when your mother dies (and a woman writes about it) that is 'emotional'? When a deprived black person is written about by a black person, that's 'universal', but when you, as a woman, write about deprived women, that is 'personal, emotional'. When I write a poem about Nicaragua (from third or fourth-hand experience) that's good, but a poem of the blood is considered 'personal'. Why is life outside, 'life', but life inside, 'not life'. If I write as a dead soldier's wife, that is invalid, if I write as someone unrelated to it, then it is a valid poem. Relationships are what keep the world going; when they are between individuals that is not valid, but when they are between countries, territories, that is 'valid'?

This goes to the heart of the differences in perception and relation to the world by women. Different worlds require different words. Women's lives *are* different; theirs is a world where intimacy is 'key in a world of connection where individuals negotiate complex networks of friendship, minimize differences, try to reach a consensus....'[2] Men live in a world of status, where 'independence is key, because a primary means of establishing status is to tell others what to do, and taking orders is a marker of low status.[3] Though all humans need both intimacy and independence, women tend to focus on the first and men on the second.' 'These differences can give women and men differing views of the same situation.... Because men and women are regarding the landscape from contrasting vantage points, the same scene can appear very different to them....'[4]

Women live very much in an 'inside' world, especially in India, where relationships, connection and the static landscape of the home pervade their experience of the world. Men (and the male world in India especially) say that experience is not of equal value with the world outside, so the writing that comes out of that world is limited, constrained, etc., i.e., not equally valid. Yet it is this very world to which they as men tenaciously cling and whose virtues they extol, deploring its apparent 'loss' in the West. To be accepted in what is essentially the man's world of literature, a woman must 'write like a man', thereby eradicating what she is as a woman. While women everywhere make the effort, and often succeed, for the sake of their survival, in understanding the language and perceptions of men (rather the way the colonized must understand the colonizer), men seem not to feel a like obligation to understand the language and perceptions of women.

If what you are as a poet is the result of what you are in all the aspects of your life—you *can't* write like a man, unless you are a (counterfeit) man. If, as Rajani Parulekar has suggested, there are social limitations on what women can 'see', can 'say', there is certainly a limitation or at least, socialization in regard to *how* women may say it. This is true everywhere, but especially in Indian society, with its restrictions on overt negative expression by women.

The social expectations for women are different. A woman is trained not to express anger or dissatisfaction, offer strong opinions on anything, speak directly, or too obviously demand anything. The question is whether women's poetry somehow reflects the institutional socialization of women's language use, or if their very perceptions of the world are so different as to pervade their use of language.

There is no hard or fast rule, but generally men's poetry is direct, and action-oriented, i.e., poems often begin with the verb (action) of the sentence; women's poetry, on the other hand, frequently begins with environment, the establishment of a mood appealing often to the senses—smell, sound (Oriya women's poetry is filled with expressions of ragas[5] as points of reference for the inner landscape, for example), texture and touch, only then going on to describe movement, action. This could, of course, be equally 'socialization' as it could be some innate orientation to or perception of the world.

Men burst upon a scene, move through a landscape, speak their minds in a meeting or group, while women, confined largely to the four walls of home, lacking 'permission' to speak in a forthright manner, or to burst in upon anything, remain an integral part of a landscape.

However, such socialization sometimes confers benefits of perception of a scene that being an outside male would not afford, as in Kirti Chaudury's *Contentment* or Savitri Rajeevan's *The Day*. Both deceptively simple scenes where minute external details which would probably rarely be noticed by a man are used to convey deep-felt, inner landscapes.

For women, there is, as Eunice de Souza has said, a battle to validate their material to begin with. Women's lives, concerns, ideas (when they dare express them) are not considered part of the so-called 'real' world; by which is meant, of course, the world inhabited and ruled over largely by men. But though many Indian women poets are shy and retiring in their public personae,[6] they turned out to have strong ideas about the real worth of women when in safe privacy with other women. Quite a number of poets said that women were 'better' poets than men because they are more faithful to their experience and feelings; others noted that if the male ego prevents men from tolerating women poets, if society doesn't take women's poetry seriously, because it does not respect women, still if you have written something which is true to life, then it will survive. Women are as 'universal' as men—but not taken seriously because of men's egoism. 'The ego of a man doesn't allow him to change or improve his thinking,' Pravasini Mahakud added. 'Women's feelings are universal; the male ego restricts men from acknowledging that women can think!'

Ironically, the largely male establishment—publishers, newspapers, poetry societies, magazines, the Sahitya Akademis (the literary academies), etc.—tends to be interested primarily in women confining themselves to publishing 'women's' topics—the very 'emotional' subject matter that they then disparage as being all that women write about. If women write about nuclear war, political issues and power, men are less comfortable. Thus,

In Their Own Voice

women are damned if they do, damned if they don't!

I was frequently asked: why an anthology of only women? mostly by men, but by a few women poets, who felt, after all, poets are poets. Some, with real hostility, said they did not want to be known as 'women poets', just poets. Jaya Mehta, for example, notes, 'There are differences in upbringing and hindrances for women. The structure of society hinders women; we need *full* equality—we are *not* different and should be treated that way. All over the world women are treated like second-class citizens.'[7] This argument, that a poet is a poet, was voiced by some older women poets who had somehow 'made the grade' (i.e., were accepted [or tolerated] by men poets, even if not on an equal footing), and by the occasional young female poet, who sought to be accepted by the *real* poets, i.e. 'men', one or two of them going so far as to dissociate herself overtly from other women poets in their languages. They were, in effect, reacting to the kind of criticism generally levelled at women 'poetesses'— that they are somehow less worthy, less real, less 'universal', than their male counterparts. And knowing too that 'poetess' is never taken as seriously as 'poet', they revel in being the only female in a bevy of males, as somehow being consequently 'worthy'. Their reality is confirmed by basking in the male presence. They are truly afraid of being 'female' and segregated as 'female', and rightly so. It is certainly a defensible and compelling reaction to the devaluation of their work as women, as has been amply demonstrated in the past.

'Some women fear, with justification, that any observation of gender differences will be heard as implying that it is women who are different—different from the standard, which is whatever men are. The male is seen as normative, the female as departing from the norm.' And the justified fear is that it is not far from 'different' to 'worse'.[8]

Thus, the answer to 'why only women poets' is primarily (though not exclusively) social, or political, rather than literary. In the many anthologies of ostensibly male and female poets of India, whether writing in English or other languages, for every 100 poets represented, at most, two or three will be female.[9] It is as if the powers that be, the 'academies', do not/cannot see or

In Their Own Voice

hear those *other* voices, female voices. They have not been sensitized to notice those voices as valid though those other voices abound. The style of women's poetry, aside from those idiosyncrasies which obtain in the work of each individual poet, (male or female), is frequently 'different', but, as this volume will testify, equally and wonderfully valid.

There is, of course, a danger inherent in dividing into categories, of any sort. Patterns of similarity are of interest, but it is offensive and misleading to reduce an individual to a category. Dividing women and men into categories risks reinforcing such reductionism. This is especially true as regards 'women'. Perhaps this will be clearer if we were to go back to those many anthologies which purport to represent all categories of, e.g., Indo-English poets, and rename them for what they really are—'An Anthology of Indian Men Poets,' or 'Indo-Anglian Male Poetry'.

On the other hand, the risk of ignoring all differences is greater than the danger of naming them. Sweeping something under the rug doesn't make it go away. Denying real difference only compounds the problem. Pretending that women and men are the same hurts women, because the ways they are regarded are based on the norms for men. The assumptions, values, and style of language that reflect and validate the writings of male poets undercut and demean women's writing.

There *are* gender differences in ways of speaking, and we need to identify and understand them. Without such understanding, we are doomed to misunderstand and undervalue the poetic style of 'the other', damaging our perception of our contrasting conversational, and consequent written styles.

ON THE ISSUE OF LANGUAGE: THEIR OWN VOICE

So many of the poets interviewed came back again and again to one particular issue—as Nita Ramaiya puts it—'trying to find the language which takes into account "ordinary" domestic life within poetry, making use of the "mundane" and churning poetry from it.' Her own poetry consciously aims to invent a woman's language, a woman's syntax and vocabulary.

'Poetry,' says Gauri Deshpande, 'is after all, an "artifice", part skill and part work. Especially (but not exclusively) in India, women don't express themselves.' And many poets like Sanghamitra Mishra, put forth the view that, 'This is necessary; our poetry is shadowed; they are writing to speak out in some way. But a woman is bound by society.' Another poet has said: 'Men underestimate women; women have no say about anything, even in the family; why would they have much of a say in the Sahitya Akademi? In my village of 250 families I was the only girl to go to college!'

Gauri Deshpande observes that, 'Men have an idea or image implanted in their heads that they have to be concerned with "important" ideas, issues. Men are more interested in being clever and are more playful. Women seem to be angry with the language itself! Possibly because the language is handed to them by men! Forced to use a language (and a "hidden" way of writing) they perhaps don't want to use, they sometimes end up using tortuous language to express simple subjects because of this.'

Filmmaker/poet Beheroze Shroff's strongly-worded views reflect a current of thought that ran through many of the statements by poets from many different areas, writing in different languages. We need a language, she says:

> to expose the lives women have been living. There is a constant trivialization of women in India, whatever they do, but the whole area of experience that males have not touched and have refused to consider is important (e.g. the unpaid labour of motherhood). But [women poets are frequently]... dealing with anger against a world which brutalizes women, whether it's the space being taken away from them on the streets, or the mental/psychological space taken from them (e.g. you are always expected to do your 'duties' as a daughter, wife etc.), so that women themselves have had difficulty taking themselves seriously as writers. This is reinforced by men's discomfort with too much truth.
>
> We need to stop seeing each other through men's eyes (and language!); we have to have a different 'women's voice' speaking to *our* problems in a phallocentric society.

We have to 'invest the language with our own authentic

meanings, insist on our own forms of language use'.[10]

Even Padma Gole, daughter of a noble, well-to-do family in Pune, speaks passionately of the lack of personhood, angry that no one thought of her as a person, as a human being. 'My poetry tried to establish that a woman was more than just a sex object, mother, wife, the sacrificing person in the family.' A role.

Lyricist Sanjeevani Marathe went so far as to say, 'A woman actually surpasses a man when she becomes "universal", i.e., goes beyond her own individual pain to the truth, the heart of a subject. Since woman is *allowed* fewer experiences in the outside world, no one knows what she is—her real essence!' Sarita Padki adds: 'The formation of personality is necessarily different for a woman, thus it must change the way a woman writes and sees; and this is valid in itself! Women need to be more faithful to their experiences, to their life as it really is. To speak in their own voice.'

One outcome of the search for a true voice is the attempt (both overt and covert) by some women poets to write in a deliberately 'anti-poetic', almost prosy style in order to overcome the expectation that women will continue to write in the 'sweet' (sometimes saccharine) voice of the 'poetess'. Certainly, the stark work of Marathi Dalit poet, Jyoti Lanjewar, the deliberately monotonous, *non*-sung, *non*-rhythmic Malayalam of Savitri Rajeevan, or the intentionally 'shocking' subject-matter of poets such as Nita Ramaiya, Eunice de Souza, Kamala Das, Jyotsna Milan, Sunanda Tripathy, Popati Hiranandani, Katyayani, or Rajani Parulekar are expressions of this attempt to break through the traditional expectations regarding women poets in India.

That women need to find their own voice was expressed over and over again, especially by poets such as Beheroze Shroff, Shanta Shelke, Nita Ramaiya, Eunice de Souza, Gagan Gill, Nabaneeta Dev Sen. That women needed to show their own face, not someone else's, whether society's, the face that men desired, the face you dared to show.... Women's poetry must above all, be a discovery of truth.

WHO ARE THE WOMEN POETS?

When I began collecting material for this anthology in 1988, and

In Their Own Voice

later on through 1989-90, I visited Sahitya Akademis and associated scholars and 'literati', and wrote countless letters to literary contacts throughout India to ask with which prominent women poets in each language I should begin my collections and interviews. Except for Marathi and Bengali, with long-standing and contemporary traditions of women poets, the answers were similar. 'Oh, there are no good modern women poets—in Telugu, in Tamil, in Hindi, in . . .' etc. Needless to say, the poetic 'establishment', whether of the Sahitya Akademis, the poetry societies, or the individual poets of repute, were invariably men. They would, invariably, bring out the names of the few well-known 'poetesses'. These women were 'known' because of the notoriety of their themes, life, or language (e.g. Kamala Das, Eunice de Souza, Malika Amar Shaikh, Mallika Sengupta, Amrita Pritam), or because through luck, fortuitous connections, or in some cases, sheer determination, their poetry had managed to secure some sort of place in this largely male-dominated sphere. That is not to say that most of these women were not good poets, and indeed, most are represented in this collection as well, but that rather, the very few women, brought out again and again, were the only ones about whom such sources seemed to have any knowledge. The disparaging comments—even about such prominent women poets—were similar as well. It was as if putting together such an anthology of 'women' was an amusing aberration, only to be expected of this strange 'western' woman.

But most of the women poets were not notorious in some way, they were mostly middle-class and educated, (as might be expected), although I made it a point to find poets from many backgrounds, and include as wide a variety of backgrounds in terms of class, caste, community and language as possible. Many of the women were married, some were not. Many of the women came from traditional backgrounds, and on the surface seemed to be typical Indian women. Some were happily married, some unhappily, some separated, some single but nearly all had something to say, and had a passionate need to question, wonder, and observe which formed an integral part of their make-up.

A few were happy in their traditional roles: Nayana Jani, a mystic poet in Gujarati, whose non-traditional marriage, non-traditional home, non-traditional views on education belied her otherwise 'traditional' stance that poets were poets, male or female; Gita Parikh, who confessed that it was very hard to write at midnight when all the work of the house was done, in spite of her apparent contentment at home. Savitri Rajeevan is a devoted, caring mother, but like Malika Amar Shaikh, Gauri Deshpande, and Mallika Sengupta, also fiercely independent in an untraditional marriage (or like the undauntable Amrita Pritam, non-marriage) across caste or community lines.

Some were determined never to marry so as to be able to write without hindrance—Rajani Parulekar, Saroop Dhruv, Pravasini Mahakud, and grand old lady, Popati Hiranandani, before them. All of them are bright, courageous, shining lights; some positively brilliant luminaries, accomplished, like Thilakavathi, Mrinal Pande, Rajee Seth, and Imtiaz Dharker, in other fields.

In my travels throughout India, I consistently met warm, live, sensitive, intelligent, articulate people; every one of these women had a story, a point of view, a spark worth igniting, worth presenting. Each, in her own way, articulated the poignant drama of contradiction that it is to be a woman of intelligence, a woman of parts. Indeed, the greatest pleasure in putting together this volume was meeting the women themselves.

There is the question of who does and who does not appear in this volume. Unfortunately, a number of poets, for some (e.g. Hiraben Pathak) no appropriate translations were available, who I would have liked to consider for inclusion either did not respond or responded too late to have good translations made of their work (e.g. O.V. Usha and Vijayalakshmi). One or two others, who for whatever reason, sometimes because they did not wish to appear in a volume exclusively devoted to the work of women, simply did not submit any or submitted only minimal examples of their work.

Certain poets, such as the Chhayavad poet, Mahadevi Varma, who conceivably could be considered to fall within the timespan of post-independence modern poets, as well as certain nineteenth century and early twentieth century poets such as Sarojini Naidu, and other poets, wonderful poets, such as Meera, and Akka Mahadevi, have been excluded based not only on time period but also on the conviction that, writing in totally traditional styles and on traditional subjects, they do not fall under the rubric of contemporary or even 'modern' poetry. I necessarily leave the exposition of their fascinating work to future volumes by other anthologizers.

Nor have I been able (as a result of inaccessibility—and/or the consequent vagaries of the mails—to various areas because of unrest, or outright war) to include many poets from languages such as Assamese or Punjabi, or any at all from Kashmiri or Rajasthani.

In the end, a conscious decision was made regarding the allotment of highly finite space in the volume—rather than tantalize the reader with just a sip of the wine of a great many poets of varying quality, with perhaps only a single poem each to represent their work, an attempt was made to lavish the reader's cup with a full draught, to choose among the best, the most prolific, representing their sometimes lifelong work by a selection from among their poems. The volume, however, is not limited by any means only to those poets, well-known in their languages; rather, a goodly amount of the spice of younger voices has been sprinkled throughout the volume. It is my fervent hope that in spite of the extreme limitations on space, this volume represents a balanced view of the contemporary work being done in India by its large and diverse contingent of women poets.

Thus, the poets in this volume represent not only those well-known in their respective languages, but those discovered by the very means women have always used, via each other, through word of mouth, through the tap root to women's underground rivers, through women's organizations, magazines, individual knowledge, and so on.

I do not claim this to be an exhaustive collection; however, it attempts to represent a wide spectrum of language, viewpoint, style, age, and repute. I have included expatriate Indian poets such as Uma Parameshwaran (Canada); Chitra Divakaruni, Ketu Katrak, Jaya Prabha, Panna Naik (USA); Sujata Bhatt (Germany); Melanie Silgardo, Shanta Acharya, and Ketaki Kushari Dyson (UK) as well. Except for the well-known (and well-accepted within India) Margaret Chatterjee, because of restrictions on

In Their Own Voice

space, I have not included naturalized Indians of foreign extraction who currently reside in India.

With such an 'embarrassment of riches' how does one go about choosing for an anthology such as this? Throughout the selection process I have tried to strike a happy balance between primarily, quality, and secondarily, fair representation.

Although I myself consider so-called 'feminist' (i.e., pro-woman, but not anti-male) themes and ideas important, I wanted to be able to present a cross-section of the work actually being written by women in India. I did not wish to bring my own—foreign—vision and orientation to the forefront so as to prejudice what I was hearing. On the other hand, I did not want merely to be influenced by establishment/male/acceptable-by-society assessments of what was or was not 'good' poetry. I truly wanted to present Indian women poets 'in their own voice'. For this reason, extensive interviews were carried out personally with as many women poets as I could meet over a fourteen-month period, to hear what these women were really thinking about themselves, about their poetry, about their place in the literary scheme of things and so on. What emerged was both congruity and variety, disguise and veracity. Congruity in that many of the same concerns were expressed again and again regardless of area, language, or even age of the poet. The variety, disguise and veracity speak for themselves within the individual poems.

In the end, I tried to choose poems primarily based on quality and wide (but fair) representation of the work being done in the various languages thematically as well as technically. However, poems concerned with 'non-modern' themes, for example, merely a reflection of early (e.g. Bhakti) traditions—i.e., concerned primarily with themes of religious devotion and ecstasy rather than with the more 'modern' issues of relationship/personhood/self-exploration/political and social consciousness, were not included even if they appeared in the post-independence period.

Then, too, there is always the element of the subjective on the part of any editor of any such work in choosing selections. Thus, subject matter, personal taste, and even point of view did enter into the selection process. I have, however, tried to maintain a

In Their Own Voice

balance throughout the volume, and also to use poetry representative of a particular poet, wherever possible (and warranted), including two or more examples of work by prolific and older poets with a large variety of work over a period of years. Occasionally, where a language has few poets and a younger poet shows great promise I have included more of her work as well.

THE TRANSLATIONS

The translations in the volume are as varied as the poets and the translators combined. As editor and as translator, I have tried to bring to the volume some element of consistency, some way, as Dryden once noted, to make the poet speak 'such English as [she] would [herself] have spoken' if she were a contemporary poet writing in largely, though not exclusively, American English. As an American I did not feel it would be appropriate for me to edit a mimicked British English, for example, and certainly not the nineteenth century Welsh English which largely forms the base for various versions of Indian English. Nor did I want the translations to parody some version of Indian English, though I have liberally interspersed as much of the original images, feel, items of Indian life, botany, cuisine, ideas etc., as would possibly be understood by the non-Indian English speaker or reader.

Generally, translations done jointly by two translators—one a native speaker of the original language, the other a native speaker of English, but both having some proficiency in the other language—seem to be the most faithful and best-crafted. When the translators are themselves poets as well, the improvement is fourfold.

I have done the greater part of the translations from Hindi and Oriya in collaboration with notable translators such as Mrinal Pande, Aruna Sitesh and J. P. Das, and in a few isolated cases in languages such as Punjabi, Maithili, Dogri, Bengali, Marathi and even Telugu, I have contributed to the translation in a variety of ways. In all such translations, I have been concerned primarily with making sure that insofar as possible the translation reflects the original, by producing in the English the same effect, the same 'sound-look', the same tone, the same 'register', the same texture as in the original. As Ramanujan notes,[11] 'only the literal text, the word made flesh, can take us to the word behind the words....'

I have tried to retain the flavour of the language of the original,[12] the Indian ambience (through use of Indian language names for things whenever this enhances rather than detracts from the meaning), and the design and style of the lines insofar as this is feasible in English. I have been particularly concerned to keep faithfully to the level of language used in the original poem; not, as so often is the case in translation into English within India, to turn colloquial, informal, everyday Oriya, Hindi, Bengali etc. into 'bookish' or 'archaic' nineteenth century or early twentieth century English, the frozen legacy of the British in India. But, it has also been my intention that each translation stands on its own in English as a poem, not merely as a translation.

For the poems which have been translated by others, I have edited all material in order to assure that those poems as well conform to such criteria of modern English. Poems in English, for the most part, appear as they were submitted. Poems in original English are in their original Indian, American or British English forms.

ACKNOWLEDGEMENTS

And finally, this anthology would never have been completed without the help, the love, the care and sometimes literally, feeding, the encouragement and support of so many people. First, I am indebted to the many friends and colleagues in India who helped me to make contact with poets in their areas and lavished hospitality and friendship: in Delhi, Romila Thapar, Aruna Sitesh, Qurratulain Hyder, Amrita Pritam, Mrinal Pande, and Lakshmi Kannan and especially to Pravin and Anita Mehta; in Bombay, Nissim Ezekiel, Eunice de Souza, Popati Hiranandani, Meenakshi and Vasant Moon, and Urmila Pawar; in Pune, Asha Mundlay, Mahadev Apte, Eleanor Zelliott, and Vidya Bal; in Kerala, Ayyappa Paniker, Kamala Das, Chandrika Balan, and

K. M. George; in Karnataka, my beloved old friends, Sulochyana and Debi Prasanna Pattanayak, as well as Anupama Niranjana, Pratibha Nandakumar and Shashi Deshpande; in Hyderabad, C. Rama Rao, Ayesha Mahmood Farooqi, Probal Das Gupta, Bh. Krishnamurti, Susie Tharu and 'Anveshi'; in Tamil Nadu, Kokilam Subbiah, Martha Ann Selby, Lee and Linda Weissman, Dr A. Manavalan, and D. Dilip Kumar of Cre-a publishers; in Gujarat, Bharat Pathak, Meena Pathak and Hasmukh Pathak; in Calcutta, Carolyne Wright and Paramita Banerjee; in Orissa, Khageswar Mahapatra, Pranati Mohanti, J. M. Mohanty, Sanghamitra Mishra, Subhendu Mund, and Sulekha Samantaray. To Jayakanta Mishra, and Anjani K. Sinha for Maithili. And, of course, my deepest thanks and love to my friends for all their advice, counsel, and handholding, J. P. Das, Gagan Gill, Usha and Anjani Sinha, Sujatha Mathai, Manisha and Shekhar Mundlay, Valerie Gauthier, Suzanne Rohe and Janet Chawla in India, and in the US and Europe, Joan Erdman, Ranjana Siddhanta Ash, Sujata Bhatt, Krishna and S. M. Pandey, Barbara and Peter Wolter, and to Christine Perri, whose letters with that incorrigible sense of humour sustained me, especially in the dark times. Further, I am utterly indebted to the wonderful, 'classy' people at USEFI (Fulbright) without whose hard work and help, I could not have made many of the contacts, appointments etc.: to Sharada Nayak, to all of them, but especially, and with great fondness, to Geeta Nayar and Uma Dasgupta. I am indebted, primarily to the Fulbright Foundation (1989-90), and additionally, to the American Institute of Indian Studies (1990) for grants which allowed me to carry out the research, translation and interviews in India for this anthology.

For their reading of and insightful comments on drafts of the manuscript in its various incarnations, I would like to thank Aditya Behl, Joan Erdman, Lisa Grayson, Christine Perri and Martha Ann Selby. However, all misdemeanors, omissions (and commissions), flights of fancy, and stray flashes of temper are my own and should not affect their karma.

Chicago, April 1991   Arlene R. K. Zide

Notes And References

1. This volume represents the culmination of two and a half years of research, interviews, translation, and collection of material from Indian women poets, a group with which the West is scarcely acquainted and many of whom are under-represented or even unknown within India as well.
2. Deborah Tannen. *You Just Don't Understand: Women and Men in Conversation.* Morrow: New York (1990), 13-17.
3. A woman's status in India is usually determined by her ability to take on her husband's (or father's) status and to order around others (usually women) below her in the pecking order.
4. *Ibid.* 26-27, 38.
5. Indian melodic lines, composed from musical scales; each raga evokes a particular time and/or season (e.g., morning raga, evening raga, monsoon raga etc.)
6. In a number of interviews with women poets, especially if the woman's English was weak or halting, her husband would become impatient and take over the conversation, speaking for her. When it was suggested that it was important that the interviews be carried out with the women, 'in their own voice', the husband was often miffed that only an accurate rendering of what the poet was saying was really required of him, considering it perfectly natural for him to *do the talking* for his wife. If, as in one instance, the wife agreed that she could be more forthcoming in the exclusive company of women, and asked him to leave the room, the husband became offended and proceeded to clatter dishes in the next room all throughout the interview. In another instance, one husband, a well-known writer in his own right, could not really understand why I wished to interview only his wife and would call again and again to ask when I was going to interview *him* ....
7. She went on to say, '"Feminist" theory just helps to separate women from men,' blaming the analyzers of the situation rather than blaming the creators of the situation. She did not consider who benefited from the situation.
8. Tannen, 13-16.
9. It is difficult to know the actual current ratio of women to men poets writing in India, partially because women writers are so much in the shadows. In Tamil, for example, the only woman poet I was referred to turned out to be the wife of a well-known movie star/political star; she wrote lyrics which were somewhat popular, but not poetry

as such. The Sahitya Akademi seemed unaware of at least two poets within its own library (unearthed for me by a [female] Tamil librarian at the Akademi who was incensed by the offhand dismissal by a male colleague, who had remarked that there were 'no good Tamil women poets' writing currently) in response to my queries. Further digging (through less established sources) revealed four other women poets of quality and about six others. While there are no doubt far more male Tamil poets writing, their work is equally mixed in quality.

10. Spender, Dale. 1991, *Man Made Language*, p. 5.
11. *Speaking of Siva*. Penguin: Middlesex. (1973). 13ff.
12. In a language such as Malayalam, this has proven to be the most difficult, first because the poetry is sung, even in the contemporary medium, and second, because the cadence and rapid, multisyllabic onomatopoeia in poems such as Sugathakumari's *The Rain At Night* are virtually impossible to capture in a language as different as English. Savitri Rajeevan's work, too, which in the Malayalam is essentially the antithesis to the usual 'poetic' (i.e., highly rhythmic, sung) style, may be seen to be a deliberate deviation and consciously 'anti-poetic' style. While the meaning and 'modern idiom' feel of the original comes through quite well in English, the deliberately monotonous tonality and line-lengths are not really reproducible in English.

IN THEIR OWN VOICE

SHANTA ACHARYA

A GIDDY MANNEQUIN

A giddy mannequin discreetly naked
I pose for you in a glass cage,
Out of your reach, perfect and undefiled.

I learnt the use of facades
When you began destroying my porcelain dolls
So long treasured behind the purdah of my self.

Dead images and my mirrors in pieces
I strive to escape continually
The incarnation of my several selves
Strewn casually over our encounters in time.

They glisten into life mocking me at multiple angles
As I puppet-dance to your discordant tunes.
I pretend not to take notice of such things.

Even this discerning unconcern
I stole from your eyes unaware,
Perfected to an art of survival

As you, in perpetual ambush,
Prefer to remove your glasses
Before you come forward to splinter mine.

I have nothing to be sad about
As our images crackle and drag.
My body remains silent and complete,
A giddy mannequin discreetly naked.

INDRANI AIKATH-GYALTSEN

THE WIDOWER

He went into the room where the coffin lay,
Moved a hairbrush an inch to the left
With some surprise, as if
His movements were divorced from his hands.
As if they were related to the objects touching them
Only in the way that two flies
Blowing and blundering in space are related
To the china and mahogany world.

The accomplished is very opposed
To the contemplated fact.
'I am free now,' said he.
He had said it many times since
The moment he suspected his wife's silence,
Realized that the bitch had died in her sleep
He left the prospect of freedom unexplored.

It was less from a feeling of remorse than
From not knowing what to do with the gift.
Anything more concrete, he would have wrapped
In tissue and laid in a drawer,
Knowing at the back of his mind—it was there,
It was his, something to possess for life.
But now—freedom?
The antithesis of stuff or glass
Possesed him to the detriment of grief.
He could not mourn like others who
Would cry for the dead until
They had appeased the world and
Exhausted what they understood
To be sorrow.
The white of his love was smudged with hate,
The black of his hate with habits knotted tight.

MEENA ALEXANDER

HOUSE OF A THOUSAND DOORS

This house has a thousand doors
the sills are cut in bronze
three feet high
to keep out snakes,
toads, water rats
that shimmer in the bald reeds
at twilight
as the sun burns down to the Kerala coast.

The roof is tiled in red
pitched with a silver lightning rod,
a prow, set out from land's end
bound nowhere.
In dreams
waves lilt, a silken fan
in grandmother's hands
shell coloured, utterly bare as the light takes her.

She kneels at each
of the thousand doors in turn
paying her dues.
Her debt is endless.
I hear the flute played in darkness,
a bride's music.
A poor forked thing,
I watch her kneel in all my lifetime
imploring the household gods
who will not let her in.

In Their Own Voice

NO MAN'S LAND

The dogs are amazing
sweaty with light
they race past the dungheaps

Infants crawl
sucking dirt from sticks
whose blunt ends
smack of elder flesh
and ceaseless bloodiness

The soldiers though
are finally resting
by the river
berets over their noses.

Barges from the north
steam past nettles
cut stalks of blackthorn
and elder, olive trees
axed into bits

Women wash their thighs
in bloodied river water,
over and over
they wipe their flesh

In stunned
immaculate gestures,
figures massed with light.

They do not hear
the men
or dogs or children.

MALIKA AMAR SHAIKH

MEGALOPOLIS 1

One whole woman
Complete with a uterus
                      One whole monsoon
                      One whole summer
                      One sky and one shore
You come to her bosom and thighs to look for the meaning of the world
Or the answers to your questions
Or just to kill time
Or for variety ....
Wife, mistress, whore
What's the difference
Unless it's only a question of statistics
You know there's more to them than their bodies
And yet you deliberately deny it
Is bed really the answer to every question?
Or is it just a reflex action?
Intercourse over, you turn your back on her and go to sleep
You don't even know then whether you're sleeping, next to a woman
a graveyard or dung
I'm surprised and not a little saddened
That in spite of it all
You can still talk about poetry

This verbal haemophilia
These phony crowns
These toys of fine sentiments
How far will they take you?
Rounding a woman's thigh
Your boats go full sail towards some ideal or the other.
Waving the uterus like a handkerchief, the women mutter
'Poor chap, we hope he finds his island'
And once again they become the third shore
or the horizon, or a little bird on a mast,
Sometimes you land on the tip of a nipple and start shouting
'Amerika Amerika' 'Eureka Eureka'
Or words to that effect

Her hair an ocean of flux
You hang your bodies to dry on her eyelashes and on her lips
Campfires of crisp and scrumptious debates
The fattened pig of ego cooking in its own juice of complacency
Spread by your sense of achievement
And you guys are really happy, you think you've got it made . . .
I never said a woman is God or something
But I think you need her
As a cover up
for your half-naked bodies

(translated from Marathi by Arun Kolatkar)

MEGALOPOLIS 9

he said write a poem on my hair
i said i'd rather write one about the human being
that's supposed to exist
somewhere between hair
and dust
only barbers and pubescent boys are obsessed by hair
and can go on talking, for hours
on whether to cut it or let it grow

do you contain the kinds of distances
the wild horses of what i want to say require
a warning
they may leave a permanent scar
on the steppes of your soul
i'd like to write about the old cotton carder
who went by a moment ago
twanging the bowstring on that instrument of his
and shaking all over
the very hair on his body resonating
as if the string he was plucking was made from his own guts

existence, all said and done, is a leaky cookpot
and yet i'll put it on the stove if you say so

somewhere along the way we've lost our language

what makes it worse is
it doesn't even matter to us any more
and you say write a poem on my eyes
write one on my lips

all the meanings in this country
this society this
city
are shepherding me towards
what
where are they taking me

i have no need of companionship any more
i've already forgotten what food is supposed to taste like
or youth for that matter
forgotten the fragrance of raw meat
and the fragrance of fresh milk

and you're telling me to write on youth

sure
there are quite a few things i could be writing about
but wait
the calf of language has been missing
and i can't find it anywhere
in the meanwhile
take this handful of words
and follow me
scatter them around like seeds

all we have to do now is give it a little time
we'll know that youth is ripe
and ready for reaping
when we hear the golden rustle of suffering

that's when i'll be able to write
on anything and everything
with sincerity
be patient
until then

(translated from Marathi by Arun Kolatkar)

BALA

from YOU AND YOU—ME AND ME

The waves on the wet beach
Adjust and shape their clothes
Unconsciously,
I keep on walking.
I rejoice at every step
Thinking I've achieved something
With each footprint.
But, adjusting their clothes
The waves
Just sweep them off
As trivialities.

YOU AND I

I walk towards the beach
The sands lay back
In stoic silence.
The waves toss about,
Heaving in anger against
The sullen sands.
The souls of the sand and sea
Lay back, expansive.
This is the place which tells you
What life is all about.
For a while,
I flew out of my small cage
To lay back like sea
And sand
Dissolving human differences.

(translated from Tamil by Lakshmi Kannan)

BALAMANI AMMA

AT THE POND

The glow of the scarlet sun
Seeped down
Into the hollows of the serpent-grove.
The tender *ilanyi* in full bloom within that fearful jungle.
Nearby, a pond
where one morning sister
And I went to bathe.
Behind us, homespun towel and small cup of sesame oil in hand,
Followed the servant-girl,
A thin figure wrapped in a tattered cloth,
A little girl with trembling eyes,
A thirteen-year-old innocent.

Many a fish circled around
Frogs stared with their bulging eyes
Turtles lumbered from the steps
Around wet blades of grass, the butterflies danced.
We could then see
The glass house chambers of the insect tribes.
We frolicked
In the cool blue waters, under the brightness of the summer sky.

The girl picked up a handful of leaves, the *emerald stone*[*]
From the serpentine stone mound.
She crushed and strained it clear
In the corner of the towel
Lathered the green liquid into our hair,
Again and then again.

We sneered at her in our clever way
Spat out childish spite
In bitter words

---
[*] name of a plant whose leaves are used for washing hair

In Their Own Voice

> Drunks, the very old, the very young never overlook
> even the smallest mistakes

How nice! using this fresh white towel
to strain the green shampoo!
What's the use of rinsing it in water
Shouldn't we be afraid to dry our hair
In so wet a towel?
Haven't you washed the stone clean yet?
It's slippery! Hurry up!!
Stop arguing, you'll get a beating
when we tell mother on you!

The boys hurt by blows
The girls wounded just with words.

She tried hard to make us relent,
But couldn't, so she sobbed,
>   *I thought of you as younger sisters!*

You know how hot such tears can be,
Beyond endurance.
We spoke no more.
Did the demons of hell laugh
And shake their matted locks of wild cane?
There was pain—
It kept on burning day and night
Though we tried hard not to remenber—
Like watching ants get crushed beneath the tread of rushing feet.

Unconfessed guilt,
The pain that no one else can understand
Even if you were to tell—
The first sense of sin.

A few days later
Others came to pick up the broom she'd set down.

Standing by the pond I now remember her.
For how many others must she have later,
Crushed her *emerald stone*
Treating them like her younger sisters!

10

In Their Own Voice

How many courtyards, porticoes and inner halls
She must have swept and mopped twice a day!
How many plants she must have watered,
Drawing the water with her thin hands!

To how many children she must have given birth
Bringing them up, fit to be blamed for many a crime!
Only despair wherever she turns
Only anger wherever she goes.
How many lands she must've seen,
Assaulted by hunger and disease.

And, in the end, how many days she must've spent in her
                                                    thatched hut
Bent double, her skin shrunken, eyes dimmed
Groaning her hopes to death.

Where has the fearful serpent-grove now gone?
The tender *ilanyi* has shed its blossoms
Trucks and cars roar down the street.
Standing here half a century later
Looking at this nearly dried-up pond,
Why did we just now remember her?

For just a moment the mind flashed forth
Many a vivid scene
The tragedy of earthquake-scorched Koyna
Vietnam fighting its triumphant dance
If we are careless,
This beam from the searchlight
Of compassion
Will fall
Only on the most distant spot.

               (translated from Malayalam by Chandrika and Ayyappa Paniker
                                   and edited by Arlene Zide)

BANAJA DEVI

ON MY OWN GRAVE

On my own grave I place a flower
Every day.
In the light of the early dawn
I tell the rising sun
Look,
Look, the lonely person loving you
Today is turned to stone,
Only she deserves
the first ray of your rising glow.

On my own grave I place a flower
In the light of a midnight moon.
Seeing that spreading moonlight
I say,
Look,
Look, this lonely person loving you
Today is silent,
Among your scattered treasures
This, her silence
You alone deserve.

(translated from Oriya by J. P. Das and Arlene Zide)

SANGJUKTA BANDYOPADHYAY

NOT A GODDESS

In the western corner of the field, the goddess Chandi* stands with her right hand up in the air, and from her hand, as if torn off, drop shreds and scraps of straw, stone flints, dead faces of children. These days nothing looks like home anymore, at times she wishes only to tie her loose hair up in a knot. An insignificant woman wipes her turmeric-stained hands on her sari end, and furtively gathers a few hibiscus flowers, forgetting about them later. After drinking the hibiscus-blossom colour of night in the middle of the wilderness, drunk and alone, the goddess stands at the head of that forgetful woman's bed in the guise of sleep.

In the western corner of the field not a goddess, but one insignificant woman arranges withered hibiscus and endless nothingness on her sari end.

---
* another name of Durga, the most popular form, in Bengal, of the consort of Shiva. Hibiscus flowers, usually scarlet, are used in her worship.

(translated from Bengali by Paramita Banerjee and Carolyne Wright, with the author)

SHUKLA BANDYOPADHYAY

HOLDING THE HAND OF A SERIAL LOVE

Holding the hand of a serial love
I find myself suddenly here.
On a far frosted January night my mother
tamed me with the heat between her breasts.
Since then, in different places
love appears: serial, elongated,
bringing with it sounds—
red, blue, pink—dipped
in deep grace. Bringing,
wrapped in a canopy of countless fairytales,
sorrow, alone. I clap harshly,
dive into a swollen ocean—
and the source opens.
What source is this
where you have brought me only to drown?
Look, ocean merges
with my eyes, love, with your legs,
your breast. Hazed in blue
where is all my blood travelling today,
to which new source?
Within the whirlpool of a serial love
it cries, what did you give me? What
given, what received? In the dense
impassable waterfalls of the heart
its lovesongs drown. Briefly
a thousand hands flail. Sin's propositions
are quenched, and the glory
of grief. I have forgotten
the face of the one who first
touched my body

holding the hand of a serial love.
In this new mirror I am seeing,
seeing seeing only me.

HIRA BANSODE

WOMAN

She, the river,
said to him, the sea:
> All my life
> I've been dissolving myself
> and flowing towards you
> for your sake
> in the end it was I
> who turned into the sea
> a woman's gift
> is always like the sky
>> but you went on
>> worshipping yourself
>> you never thought
>> of becoming a river
>> and merging
>> with me

(translated from Marathi by Vinay Dharwadker)

LOOK, MOTHER

Look, mother,
ever since father died,
you've been badly shaken
by all the grief and fear.
Think of it this way:
the wheels of a cart
are bound to move up and down,
but all they've got to do
is grip the earth under them
as firmly as they can.
Mother, we're people
from the backwoods,
it's an old habit with us
to stitch together
our sorrows and joys with thorns.

In Their Own Voice

Don't you think we now need
to bear these wounds
without wincing?
Let go of the pain a little,
see how everything will become light.
If I have to do it,
I'll wash dishes in four more homes,
but I won't let you run short
of anything you need.
Don't cry, I'm going crazy too.
What can I do,
I've come to a strange place, haven't I,
for the sake of a living.
We live so far apart,
but it's as though your wings
were always spread over me.
You watch over me
and my burden of tiredness,
of pointless work,
grows a little lighter.
Oh—the train has blown its whistle!
Be careful on the way,
mother,
give everyone in the family
the news about me.
Stick to your plans for the journey,
and send me a letter
as soon as you get there.
Go carefully now—take care, mother, take care.

Note: Hira Bansode is a Dalit woman writer. In the original, this poem is written entirely in a common rural low-caste dialect of Marathi. Its speaker is a young Dalit woman, who has moved to the city on her own to work as a domestic servant. She is at the railway station, saying goodbye to her aging mother, who has been visiting her and is now taking a train back to their village in the country.

(translated from Marathi by Vinay Dharwadker)

NIRMAL PRABHA BARDOLOI

HE WOULD HAVE COME LONG AGO

He was to come
Along your razor-sharp vision
He was to come
Along the stream of your blood,
Through your stretched-out shrunken hands
And clenched fists.

He wishes to come
But turns back again and again
With a frown on his helpless face

He was to come
In the flickering flame of your third eye,
He was to come
In your *Bhujangasana* posture.

He wishes to come
But turns back again and again
With the mute curse of fury.

On seeing your drooping head
He turns back
Seeing you locked in momentary infatuations,
seeing your pale, blurred vision,
Your watery blood,

Your hands clenched in self-hatred,
Shrunken, unextended

He would have come long ago.

(translated from Assamese by Emdad Ullah)

In Their Own Voice

I AM THERE

Wherever you are
Shy
There grows
My
Sal tree of
Promise.
Wherever
You feel helpless
You will find
My voice —
I am there.

Dishang
Rhine
Mississippi
Thames
Everywhere
You will find me.

(translated from Assamese by Arabinda Nath Sharma)

In the smell of rice fields in autumn
My father comes back to me;
In the fragrance of the new scarf
As I unfold it fresh from the shop
I find my mother again . . .

Where shall I leave myself
For my child
O, where indeed?

(translated from Assamese by Hiren Gohain)

ANJANA BASU

YELLOW

He lives in a yellow room.
A tree points to him and sputters
pink messages that smell of flowers.
A bird sits on my finger and sings
about him and builds a nest
and raises a family of singing birds
by my fingernails.
Every note in my body is a song of
a yellow room.

NO NUCLEAR NIGHT, BHOPAL

Turpentine grass grows over this cold
steel town
its black fingers lick the blue sky

and the birds ooze down drip by drip
painted out, painted dead.

One night the sky split, spat bright
blood red

colour killed us

colour killed the night

cannibal colour.

Glowing dust grows over this turpentine
town
Small birds scream at night
in dead droplets.

KRISHNA BASU

GOLD COINS

What venom have you kept concealed within your hair?
Always poised like a snake, in a posture of attack
Against your husband and other men.
You walk like a gypsy woman with your hair down
Caring for no one.

You'd gone to a place of barter
Where the price for your hair was fixed.
Paying two gold coins, an eager merchant
Bought up the lushness, venom, thrill, the key of your hair
Everything.

A henna-complexioned boy from the outskirts of Bengal
Raised his copper-coloured face to look upon your hair.
He worshipped it—once, in a kiss, and once in his lust
He never got the blue of your hair's jungle.

How much could the poor guy pay
To buy that blue length of hair?
His arms aren't long enough to buy such a graceful doll
He knows you are priceless
So never even tried to buy you.
He never did win the cloudy blue of your hair's jungle,
But the merchant did.
You're not as priceless as all that!

(translated from Bengali by Paramita Banerjee and Arlene Zide)

ISHITA BHADURI

TWENTY-SEVEN MILLION YEARS LATER

Twenty-seven million years later I'll forget:
This sunshine
The warmth rising from the veins of my navel
Secret, sinless.

Twenty-seven million years later I'll forget:
Last night
The Id-moon
Still unkissed.

Twenty-seven million years later I'll forget:
Today's beauty bath
In words and phrases of endearment.

Twenty-seven million years later
I'll forget everything
I'll get amnesia.

Twenty-seven million years later
I'll turn into a spiritless mummy
And you, a legend
In history.

(translated from Bengali by Paramita Banerjee and Arlene Zide)

SHOBHA BHAGWAT

HUSBANDS

This woman has a job
so her husband is unhappy
this one sits at home
so her husband is upset
this one is very thin
so her husband is angry
this one is very plump
so her husband snaps at her
though this one has a lovely figure
her husband is grouchy
he is troubled by doubts
and simmers all the time
this one is very talkative
so her husband dislikes her
this one is very quiet
so her husband cannot stand her
this one has a messy home
so her husband complains
this one has a spic-and-span home
so her husband is morose
this one is always well-dressed
so her husband wonders, 'For whom?'
this one is always plainly dressed
so her husband says, 'She's dumb.'
Does this tight-rope balancing act
ever come to an end?
Where can one find a husband
who likes his wife?

(translated from Marathi by Vinay Dharwadker)

AMRITA BHARATI

THE SNAKE AND THE MAN

Before, I used to be afraid of snakes.

It would often start in my dreams
Sometimes beneath the rope-string cot
Sometimes on the pillow
I used to slide along his smoothness
and fall into a chasm
and he bit me every time.

I would die a slow, slow death
Telling mother, father, everyone
How I'd been bitten by a snake.
But like machines, they
Sat frozen in their places,
Deaf, unmoved.

I wanted to go out into the neighbourhood
And then beyond the city
To the sweeper-away of poison, that witchdoctor
And to that little friend of mine
Whose bucket once had held a snake
As she pulled it from the well.

But all of this went on in some faraway scene
While my feet stood rooted to a stone.

Before, I used to fear the snake,
But now, it's man I fear.

(translated from Hindi by Mrinal Pande and Arlene Zide)

SUJATA BHATT

UDAYLEE*

Only paper and wood are safe
from a menstruating woman's touch.
So they built this room
for us, next to the cowshed.
Here, we're permitted to write
letters, to read, and it gives a chance
for our kitchen-scarred fingers to heal.

Tonight, I can't leave the stars alone.
And when I can't sleep, I pace
in this small room, I pace
from my narrow rope-bed to the bookshelf
filled with dusty newspapers
held down with glossy brown cowries and a conch
When I can't sleep, I hold
the conch shell to my ear
just to hear my blood rushing,
a song throbbing,
a slow drumming within my head, my hips.
This aching is my blood flowing against,
rushing against something—
knotted clumps of my blood,
so I remember fistfuls of torn seaweed
    rising with the foam,
rising. Then falling, falling upon the sand
strewn over newly laid turtle eggs.

WHITE ASPARAGUS

Who speaks of the strong currents
streaming through the legs, the breasts
of a pregnant woman
in her fourth month?

---
*   untouchable during menstruation

In Their Own Voice

She's young, this is her first time,
she's slim and the nausea has gone.
Her belly's just starting to get rounder
her breasts itch all day,

and she's surprised that what she wants
is *him*
      inside her again.
Oh come like a horse, she wants to say,
move like a dog, a wolf,
      become a suckling lion-cub—

Come here, and here, and here—
but swim fast and don't stop.

Who speaks of the green coconut uterus
the muscles sliding, a deeper undertow
and the green coconut milk that seals
her well, yet flows so she is wet
from his softest touch?

Who understands the logic
behind this desire?

Who speaks of the rushing tide
      that awakens
her slowly increasing blood—?
And the hunger
      raw obsessions beginning
with the shape of asparagus:
sun-deprived white and purple-shadow-veined,
she buys three kilos
of the fat ones, thicker than anyone's fingers,
she strokes the silky heads,
some are so jauntily capped . . .
           even the smell pulls her in—

MANORAMA MAHAPATRA BISWAL

MY WHOLE LIFE FOR HIM

If ever he comes under a silent sun
Dampening my eyelids
Or else in a heavy downpour
Of the month of *Shravana*
In the *behag* raga of the sarangi

How would he know
I am not here any longer.
I burn like a wound
On some missile range by the sea.

Surely, he'll come
The neem tree will have flowered
Its fragrance drifting all around.
He'll grope for a lost childhood
Will mope over it.
He won't have forgotten
That childhood like a squirrel's back,
The village childhood
Full of neem and mustard flowers.

A quiet girl like a shadow
Red-hued like the *manjistha* blossom
A sullen sunset in her eyes
Will ask about me
And of other things
But how would she know
For whom
A whole life passed,
Waiting, waiting.

(translated from Oriya by J. P. Das and Arlene Zide)

BRATATI BIWAS

THE TEMPTATION WHICH

lets me forget quite easily
the prissy temptations of coloured candles, foil-wrapped chocolates
and such
Kettledrums of light roll in the heavenly garden
The forbidden fruit flares its serpent's hood along my extended palm
What a relentless sun in the midday sky!
A cloudy sky, a sari with its border of narrow stripes,
hurt pride pinched between the brows
cherished pleasure moving in my breast
white as a conchshell, moonlight floating in birds' feathers
A bluish dream lying in fathomless water—
loving all these
this substitute museum for me seems lifeless.

This heavenly garden, disgusting
curses and insults strewn before my eyes.

A cloudy sorrow, coloured candles
or tawdry tin-foil crown abandoned in the days of childhood

throw me down, into the aggressive mouth of the netherworld.

(translated from Bengali by Paramita Banerjee and Arlene Zide)

CANTIRAKANTI

WANTED: A BROOM

when he said Darling
he didn't ask for a paisa for anything
but when he said Marry Me
he asked for gold
money
stuff
plates and pots
everything
aiyo he even asked for a broom
to sweep the floor
I said
the broom's the limit
he got up and asked why

I said
so I can sweep you from my heart
and toss you in the trash

paying a life-subscription
just to get a male hooker
what am I
half-crazy
or a total fool

(translated from Tamil by Martha Ann Selby and K. Paramasivam)

MARGARET CHATTERJEE

FROM THE ABYSS

We who have known destruction
And who were destroyed
Speak.

We of Belsen and Buchenwald,
Who loved beautiful things,
Heard the jackboot on the stairs, and the van draw up outside—
Now we are not a name, a memory.

We of Bengal too who lay in the streets
While you passed on the other side,
And grain rotted in the granaries,
We had to watch our children die—
We who would have sung songs in kinder days.

We are a large company.
We are from Coventry and the East End,
Stalingrad, Cologne, Warsaw and Caen,
Paris, Berlin, and Hiroshima,
We knew the terror by night—
The destruction at noonday.

We watch now through dark shutters.
We have no eyes but yours,
No mouth to speak, save yours.
They said we died for freedom.
Let it not be a lie.
They said it would be the last time.
Let it not be a lie.

When men clamour for new myths
Like children clamouring for tasty dishes,
Remember we heard it all before.
When people talk of a bomb
Like children of a new toything,
Remember us, you who never knew our names or saw our faces.

When rich men make poverty a virtue

In Their Own Voice

Tell them we died of hunger.
When people talk of toleration
Tell them our synagogues were smashed,
Our temples and churches desecrated.
When they talk of democracy
Tell them that some of us died in Spain
Because we cared too much.

You world-makers, lovers of towers and mountains,
Who fashion the time of day with visions,
Who are not put off with fine phrases—
We also loved the world and died in exile.
We have no voice left but yours . . . . . .

CHAITALI CHATTOPADHYAY

RAGE

One road has gone down the darkened slope
At the outset of the other sits an owl.
I've never had a home; those were all lies I told you
        to keep you from getting frightened; know that—
Neither am I human, born of a witch-mother's womb
In her eighth bearing, a vial of poison beneath my tongue.
I wander alone, drifting through the night,
And when people make magic signs and passes at me,
With both my hands, I rip away my cunt.
Fire loves me ardently, at my bidding
Has turned my pelvic joints to ashes,
I've hung the web
Of all my mystery on a dead branch of the wild *ashshyaora** tree;
Below, as today you pass this way, I will call to you no longer.

---

* a wild tree believed to be a favourite haunt of female ghosts and witches in popular superstition

(translated from Bengali by Paramita Banerjee and Arlene Zide)

GITA CHATTOPADHYAY

THE RITUAL OF SATI

The dog has crossed the knee-deep dark
    stream of water,
that trickle oozing out of your eyes
    is your Baitarani River*
Your *jamrul***-tree body covered
    with poisonous ants,
a hard fist holds you down in case you want
    to come back.
You're going to burn here, now mount
    the funeral pyre.
You're going to burn here, now mount
    the memory pyre.
You're going to burn here—bloody lips,
    navel the colour of copper.
Lift the face-cloth, take a last look
    at your husband's face.

---

* The Baitarani is a mythical river the spirits of the dead must cross to reach the afterworld, much like the Styx or the Jordan in Western mythology.

** *Jamrul* wood is often used for funeral pyre fuel.

Note: On 4 September 1987, in the village of Deorala in Rajasthan, an eighteen-year-old Rajput woman, Roop Kanwar, burned herself alive on the funeral pyre of her husband, setting off storms of controversy, and a flurry of legislation, in the country. Alleged eyewitnesses first claimed that the girl committed sati voluntarily, this being a long-revered custom for Rajput widows. Later, however, after the central and state governments voiced tardy disapproval, and sent police to close off the area to thousands of fervent pilgrims and curiosity seekers, the story emerged that the young woman was dragged to the pyre, screaming for mercy, by her in-laws who were anxious for the glory—and revenue—that have accrued to Rajasthani villages claiming a sati in their past.

(translated from Bengali by Paramita Banerjee and Carolyne Wright)

In Their Own Voice

THIRTY-FIVE PARGANAS*

A motorbike, stengun, a dazzle of black,
the one who has just fallen down on her face,
    isn't that India?
We got two harvests from our fields, not just wheat
    but gold from the mines,
now turned into sharp steel or a ball of fire.
Don't the girls come to take water
    from the Shatadru River any longer?
Cowherd, sitting on the Kaveri's banks, don't
    you let drop your long fishline anymore?
The image of the goddess stopped unfinished
    in the Ganges' clay,
watch out, the boat's about to capsize
    in the Brahmaputra's current!
Whoever you are, putting in my hands
    the shattered thirty-five districts,
shatter me also into pieces and pieces
    and pieces and pieces . . .
A motorbike, a stengun, a dazzle of black,
the one who has just fallen down on her face,
    isn't that India?

---

* Pargana: The Indian term for an administrative district. The area immediately surrounding Calcutta is a district called Chabbish Pargana (Twenty-Four Parganas).

Note: The rivers named run through the Punjab; Karnataka and Tamil Nadu in the South; the Gangetic Plain from Uttar Pradesh to Bengal; and Assam, respectively—that is, all the cardinal points of the subcontinent.

(translated from Bengali by Paramita Banerjee and Carolyne Wright)

SNEHMAYEE CHAUDHARY

THE LUCKY ONES

There was a lake
within me
which, off and on
lit up my eyes.
Everything was fine
till then.

But, from the time it froze into a block of ice
it grew very heavy,
made things difficult for me.

How lucky those
who in the winter
never let it freeze
and from the warmth within themselves
keep their own lakes flowing.

(translated from Hindi by Aruna Sitesh and Arlene Zide)

KIRTI CHAUDHURY

CONTENTMENT

Everything stays the same
These curtains . . . this window, these plants in their pots . . .
Nothing ever changes.

But what happens
Sometimes
The colours of the flowers glow.
Suddenly, the embroidery on the tablecloth and cushions
starts to smile.
The walls—just about to speak
Nearby all the scattered books
are about to open up their secrets,
word by word.

Unconsciously, a song comes to your lips.
Is this
contentment?
Nothing has changed,
but what happens, sometimes?

(translated from Hindi by Aruna Sitesh and Arlene Zide)

MAHUYA CHAUDHURY

THE TRIBE

Those who knew about her private killing ground
of the revamping of all her weapons
Their talent for encompassing has today come toppling to the ground.
Gradually, they have learnt to tell a male waterfall from a female
Going out in search of the pearl-hued drink, they have started
                                            disappearing
in hordes. Their tribal guru-jester, head and ears wrapped in a shawl,
                                         mumbles endless-
ly—
How, this being no suburb, the clay has become soft and viscous,
                                                 winter
slipping in through their rustic mud walls.
How, somehow pushing up through the knee-deep water and
                                      the filth of their scriptures
a primal epic god is born, rises,
his clumsy pattern spit out on the terrace of the sanatorium in
                                         mad fits of retching
his omnipresent fear a social watchword; they say
the witch-repelling breeze digs up someone's lock of hair.

It lasts, at most, for six lunar months —
From her arms, transparent as glass, her shelter flies off
the rites of lost worship, lust extending right up into the suburbs
suck dry the desert-land with its set of gleaming milk-teeth.
This city, as far-reaching as the sun,
gradually fades away, a bubble with its rainbow-coloured sunset
                                     paths, its design-covered walls;
Playfully, the phantom shape floats across, dashes against the
                                        banks of the canal
Its swollen belly an unbroken sphere; overhead
a thousand coins jingle in paradise, the people talk
about how, on the last path, climbing upward toward the stars,
they'd managed to craft real homes.

        (translated from Bengali by Paramita Banerjee and Arlene Zide)

BAHINABAI CHOUDHURY

LIFE

Well, life . . . yes, life
it's a wok on fire
burn your fingers
before you eat a bite.

Get on with life
and don't see what is not
you'd hardly call a spire
a tapering sort of pot!

And it is your life
don't cry and moan
a golden crown on your head
would you call it a load?

Listen, in life
as one, two decide
and say yea to sorrow
and nay to delight!

You see this life
is two folks' deal
some cash some credit
some sorrow some weal.

(translated from Marathi by Gauri Deshpande)

VIJAYA DABBE

CALL THEM WHAT YOU WILL

Ours is a palace
with glass walls
and golden cupola
The floors gleam
The pillars glisten
We haven't kept count
of Duryodhanas
who get themselves beaten.

You must
walk within
Again and again
Circle the same pillars
Then you'll see
the many-coloured dead
butterflies.

Did all this colour
Appear by itself?
Didn't it come flying in
After the pain was swallowed
The tears shed
With the blackened Urmila
Crawling into a corner?

Wasn't it within these
Age-old walls
That the toll was paid?
No matter then
If the goldsmith
Fretworked every spot
On every wing
Thousands of paired glances
Strike the eye.
People scared of

In Their Own Voice

Living creatures
Now pick the bodies up
Joyfully
Arrange them neatly
in dolls' houses.
People are frightened
when they see them flapping, dying
Unable to open their wings.
These, dying, don't utter
a word.

Flying here and there
Somehow rushing into
the coloured palace
Not finding the way out
Not seeing the glass
Trying to leap to the sky
and falling dead
Memorialized
By the Archaeology Department.

Call them
what you will.
Seeta
Draupadi
It's all the same.

(translated from Kannada by Tejaswini Niranjana)

AZIZ BANO DARAB

THE SEASON OF RAINS

Though I loved the rains no less,
I rushed inside myself
To shelter from the downpour.

But within me too, I came upon the landscape of the rains
The scene outside
I found the same within.

The torrents, truly my own emotions
The clouds had turned the day to darkness and
I felt that I had once dwelled in this very forest.

I saw some dollhouses made of sand,
A paper boat;
A *bustee** of memories sunk in the mist.
Before my eyes came
All the former births within my life
And suddenly the clouds behind my eyes began to rain.

How long this storm went on I don't know,
Demolishing this town of memory
It brought down domes and arches, niches,
The balconies and portals.
While hope's songbird went on warbling,
A broken bridge withstood the lashing torrents.

After wiping out the village of memories,
The rain lifted.
A rainbow spread across the sky.
But for a broken bridge and a waterless stream
Every other scene was washed away.
The inevitable end had come at last.
Something to marvel at!—
That even this much was left to be lost!
Who would be surprised

---

* local dwellings, slum

If tomorrow even the fields of tears
Were found to be barren,
And the clouds of my eyes were to find no sand
In the foothills of my rain-forests.

The river of dust which flows within me
Has long been recounting the tale
Of how its shores had crumbled.
Now, even the next monsoon will sweep it away, too.

The Season of Rains will find nothing
Nothing at all, nothing at all, nothing at all.

(translated from Urdu by Qurratulain Hyder and Arlene Zide)

GHAZALS

So that I may meet myself
From a river I must turn into a waterfall.

When I was growing up some well-meaning relatives
Gave me several masks and a tongue of stone.

Thoughtlessly, he turns the pages
When my face becomes a book.

Why would he take me out of myself,
Why should anyone put his hands in someone else's fire?

He keeps probing in the ashes of my past
He'll burn his fingers, if I'm not careful.

He's a weary traveller
I, a locked caravanserai
Even if he reaches me,
What will he find?

(translated from Urdu by Qurratulain Hyder and Arlene Zide)

BIJOYINI DAS

KUBUJA*

Hasn't the Konarak of my words
ever rippled the calm waters of someone's mind?
not filled them with a magical feeling
or with a magnificent utterance
full of surprise and excitement?

Hasn't the splendour of my thought
planted a sapling in some soil
fertile with an affectionate heart?
Hasn't the infant of my sympathy
placed her feet
on the arid sands
of unrelieved sorrow?

I always forget the mathematics
of loss and gain.
A foolish pupil in the village school
though I bleed
at the cane strokes of the teacher,
still I fail to grasp the arithmetic of worldliness.

I have never been miserly
about sharing the treasure of my experience
with the prince as well as with the pauper.
I have painted pictures,
like the golden footsteps of the goddess Lakshmi,
of the world's sorrow, misery, love and betrayal
on the mud walls of my mind, wiped clean.

Still, the world has not understood me.
Like a worm-eaten book, unread
I still lie in some corner of the house.
Or else, I am an oyster,
a pearl within its womb,

---

* the hunchbacked woman who turned into a beauty at Krishna's touch

In Their Own Voice

lying on a desolate seashore
measuring the distance from sunrise to sunset
the distance from cradle to burning ghat
the distance from the temple of faith
to the grave of treachery.

The fresh flower garland withers in the evening,
The morning's pestled sandalwood paste dries up in the evening.
Still, I go on stringing garlands and pestling sandalwood
                                      every morning.

The anticipation of someone's coming
goes on cooing like the pigeons
In the temple courtyards of my mind.

I feel as if there's someone all my own
In some corner of the earth.
He will come one day,
Will take away my burdens, free me
From the dark shadows of my nightmares,
From the agony of sleepless nights,
From the pale corpse of my hopes
And the corpse of brooding moments.

He will touch my motionless hands
With the warmth of countless promises.

Bent beneath the weight of
Misery, sorrow, sin
My personality will stand up straight with pride
Garland the sun
And decorate the moon with sandalpaste,
Will seek its own identity.
Surely, there is someone
Who is mine and mine alone.

(*translated from Oriya by J. P. Das, Sulekha Samantaray and Arlene Zide*)

JYOTSNA DAS

COINCIDENCE

When you meet the ocean
Your desires turn to waves
Words vaporize into air.
Taking a step forward
Your anxious thoughts flame into a pyre,
Wet feet and sand washed clean.

When you meet the forest
Your desires become the seasons
Your smiles turn into brooks
Thorn and brush drag at your feet
And the hills stop you on your way.

Out of coincidence pain is born
Coincidence is happiness,
The camel resting on the desert sands
Rises, slowly moving
Towards a sudden liberation.

The eyes' tears
Cross the shores of the lips
Dreams lie asleep
In closed rooms.
You wouldn't want to wake them
From the depths of slumber.

(translated from Oriya by J. P. Das and Arlene Zide)

KAMALA DAS

AN INTRODUCTION

I don't know politics but I know the names
Of those in power, and can repeat them like
Days of week, or names of months, beginning with
Nehru. I am Indian, very brown, born in
Malabar, I speak three languages, write in
Two, dream in one. Don't write in English, they said,
English is not your mother-tongue. Why not leave
Me alone, critics, friends, visiting cousins,
Every one of you? Why not let me speak in
Any language I like? The language I speak
Becomes mine, its distortions, its queernesses
All mine, mine alone. It is half English, half
Indian, funny perhaps, but it is honest,
It is as human as I am human, don't
You see? It voices my joys, my longings, my
Hopes, and it is useful to me as cawing
Is to crows or roaring to the lions, it
Is human speech, the speech of the mind that is
Here and not there, a mind that sees and hears and
Is aware. Not the deaf, blind speech
Of trees in storm or of monsoon clouds or of rain or the
Incoherent mutterings of the blazing
Funeral pyre. I was child, and later they
Told me I grew, for I became tall, my limbs
Swelled and one or two places sprouted hair. When
I asked for love, not knowing what else to ask
For, he drew a youth of sixteen into the
Bedroom and closed the door. He did not beat me
But my sad woman-body felt so beaten.
The weight of my breasts and womb crushed me. I shrank
Pitifully. Then . . . . I wore a shirt and my
Brother's trousers, cut my hair short and ignored
My womanliness. Dress in sarees, be girl
Be wife, they said. Be embroiderer, be cook,
Be a quarreller with servants. Fit in. Oh,

Belong, cried the categorizers. Don't sit
On walls or peep in through our lace-draped windows.
Be Amy, or be Kamala. Or, better
Still, be Madhavikutty. It is time to
Choose a name, a role. Don't play pretending games.
Don't play at schizophrenia or be a
Nympho. Don't cry embarrassingly loud when
Jilted in love .... I met a man, loved him. Call
Him not by any name, he is every man
Who wants a woman, just as I am every
Woman who seeks love. In him .... the hungry haste
Of rivers, in me .... the oceans' tireless
Waiting. Who are you, I ask each and everyone,
The answer is, it is I. Anywhere and,
Everywhere, I see the one who calls himself
I in this world, he is tightly packed like the
Sword in its sheath. It is I who drink lonely
Drinks at twelve, midnight, in hotels of strange towns,
It is I who laugh, it is I who make love
And then, feel shame, it is I who lie dying
With a rattle in my throat. I am sinner,
I am saint. I am the beloved and the
Betrayed. I have no joys which are not yours, no
Aches which are not yours. I too call myself I.

THE OLD PLAYHOUSE

You planned to tame a swallow, to hold her
In the long summer of your love so that she would forget
Not the raw seasons alone, and the homes left behind, but
Also her nature, the urge to fly, and the endless
Pathways of the sky. It was not to gather knowledge
Of yet another man that I came to you but to learn
What I was, and by learning, to learn to grow, but every
Lesson you gave was about yourself. You were pleased
With my body's response, its weather, its usual shallow
Convulsions. You dribbled spittle into my mouth, you poured
Yourself into every nook and cranny, you embalmed

My poor lust with your bitter-sweet juices. You called me wife,
I was taught to break saccharine into your tea and
To offer at the right moment the vitamins. Cowering
Beneath your monstrous ego I ate the magic loaf and
Became a dwarf. I lost my will and reason, to all your
Questions I mumbled incoherent replies. The summer
Begins to pall. I remember the ruder breezes
Of the fall and the smoke from burning leaves. Your room is
Always lit by artificial lights, your windows always
Shut. Even the air-conditioner helps so little,
all pervasive is the male scent of your breath. The cut flowers
In the vases have begun to smell of human sweat. There is
No more singing, no more a dance, my mind is an old
Playhouse with all its lights put out. The strong man's technique is
Always the same, he serves his love in lethal doses,
For, love is Narcissus at the water's edge, haunted
By its own lonely face, and yet it must seek at last
An end, a pure, total freedom, it must will the mirrors
To shatter and the kind night to erase the water.

YASHODARA DAS

DHARMAPADA*

He did not have in his hands
Chisel and hammer
To crown Konarak
He is not Dharmapada
In his hands
Is only a rickshaw handle,
Sheikh Khalil his name.
In those hands, thin as the *lauki* vine
The handle of a cycle-rickshaw.
His legs still unfamiliar
With rickshaw pedals
Unafraid of trucks and buses
He drove the rickshaw
From Jhanjirimangala to Tulsipur.

Hands that should have held paper and pen
Hands that should have held the reel of a kite
Hands that should have held brush and palette
Hands that should have held a flute
Those hands held the handle of a rickshaw.
Unafraid, he pedalled
Ten hours a day
The entire burden of his family
On his shoulders.
How could head or hands
Tackle anything but the rickshaw?
Earning ten rupees
He could buy rice and dal,
Tapioca and barley for an ailing sister,
A *burqa*** for his mother,
A woman, unallowed

---

*   the boy sculptor who was sacrificed after he fixed the crowning stone to the top of Konarak temple

** *burqa*—a veiled cloth worn by Muslim women to hide their bodies and faces

In Their Own Voice

To work outside the home
She said to her son:
    It's a man's duty to look after women,
Since his father ran away from the battlefield of life
This 12-year-old now heads the family.

Sheikh Khalil understands nothing.
This much he knows
He has to fix the crowning stone
On Konarak temple
With sweat and blood
Dragging
His rickshaw from Tulsipur to the OMP crossing.

(translated from Oriya by J. P. Das and Arlene Zide)

MAMATA DASH

MURDERER

Did I ever call you?
No, I don't think so.
But then,
Where did you come from, and why?
Suddenly blackening
The heart of those bright days I'd earned.
The long, shining knife in your hand
Pointing only at me.
I know then it's only you who are my murderer.

Let it be.
To make this unbearable life of mine, which gradually grows hotter
Worth living
I kept rearranging it all the time,
In all these,
From the constantly ending rainfalls
To the kiss which vanished in a moment
To the bed of snow which melted, in a moment.
But then, had I wanted
Somebody to murder me this way?
When I am so mauled, defeated
At the hands of unfulfilled aspirations?

Have you hung around your neck
That garland
Of all the faces that I loved, once called my own?
Then you've killed
The cuckoo's call, the moonlight, the honey, the enchantment of
                                           my world
The serpent's dance,
Killed the music of the flute
Echoing in my secret forest.
Purple blood sticking to your knife
The power of your presence shook
The very ground beneath my feet—
The drama of my past

In Their Own Voice

Shines in the mirror of your crown jewel,
You laugh, laugh on and on
My head bent
In shame, in fear, devotion
Or is it the assurance of my having final shelter.

I won't go anywhere, I promise,
So do not bind my hands and feet,
I don't know from where
This anxious wish comes, this yearning for the touch
Of your shining knife
This harsh touch of intense cruelty.
Look, something like a soft twilight
Surrounds us

Come, murderer,
Step into my sacred courtyard
You're my last guest, after all, aren't you?
Come, today I feel, you also are my final love.

(translated from Oriya by J. P. Das and Arlene Zide)

GAURI DESHPANDE

WORKADAY WOMEN

I

    In a city
there are six long mondays
when you spend your mornings
jammed up against women
sour smelling of sweat
perfume talcum soap
each bracing herself to face the files
machines pencils pupils people
slights yells lunches delays.
And evenings they are packed more dense
grimy with weariness.
Their eyes are vacant and they don't push
even to get off the train.

II

    The skin will thicken, toughen
protect you from seeing the tailless cat, his forepaw torn
the man with a gash from ear to ear sewn
with fortyseven stitches
and long ditches of water
bordered by mounds of filth
of course small children
whose sight is agony.
On six-long monday you
are pushed, pulled dully
stared at, thick, opaque.

    And the too solid flesh
will refuse
when he demands that it melt
at a saturday-touch.
You have not been protected after all
from women men children cats.

In Their Own Voice

THE FEMALE OF THE SPECIES

Sometimes you want to talk
about love and despair
and the ungratefulness of children.
A man is no use whatever then.
You want then your mother
or sister
or the girl with whom you went through school,
and your first love, and her
first child—a girl—
and your second.
You sit with them and talk.
She sews and you sit and sip
and speak of the rate of rice
and the price of tea
and the scarcity of cheese.
You know both that you've spoken
of love and despair and ungrateful children.

EUNICE DE SOUZA

POEM FOR A POET

It pays to be a poet.
you don't have to pay prostitutes.

Marie has spiritual thingummies.
Write her a poem about the
Holy Ghost. Say:
'Marie, my frequent sexual encounters
represent more than an attempt
to find mere physical fulfilment.
They are a poet's struggle to
transcend the self
and enter into
communion
with the world.'

Marie's eyes will glow.
Pentecostal flames will descend.
The Holy Ghost will tremble inside her.
She will babble in strange tongues:

'O Universal Lover
in a state of perpetual erection!
Let me too enter into
communion with the world
through thee.'

Ritu loves music and
has made a hobby of psychology.
Undergraduate, and better still,
uninitiated.
Write her a poem about woman flesh.
Watch her become oh so womanly and grateful
Giggle with her about
horrid mother keeping an eye
on the pair, the would-be babes
in the wood, and everything will be
so idyllic, so romantic
so *intime*

Except, that you, big deal,
are forty-six
and know what works
with whom.

IDYLL

When Goa was Goa
my grandfather says
the bandits came
over the mountain
to our village
only to splash
in cool springs
and visit Our Lady's Chapel.
Old ladies were safe
among their bags
of rice and chillies,
unperturbed
when souls restless in purgatory
stoned roofs
to ask for prayers.
Even the snakes bit
only to break the monotony.

NABANEETA DEV SEN

THE CHILD'S SAYING

Whenever I see you
that exiled homeless pavement-dweller
girl inside my heart, starving the whole day,
begins a tremendous uproar.
Millions of lice bite in her matted hair,
suddenly blood oozes from her chapped unoiled skin,
then her shrieks keep all the crows
        in the neighbourhood away.
Only when she sees you
only when she sees you
that senseless naked urchin in the depths of my heart
abandons all her games in the dust
and screams out hungrily—'Give me love!'
Wailing, she stretches out her arms—

Hearing this, her playmates, the streetdogs and crows
pause in their snatching games
and observe two minutes of silence
        on the garbage heap.

*(translated from Bengali by Paramita Banerjee and Carolyne Wright
with the author)*

SOMETIMES, LOVE

It comes when you call it. Like a pet cockatoo
it comes and sits on your finger. It flutters.
Swaying its neck, fluffing its feathers,
        making its topknot dance,
it recites fixed phrases. It says flattering words,
my dazzling-white bird, words
to flatter me, words it's been taught to repeat;
it pours honey into my ears.
Then, in private,
alone,

In Their Own Voice

sitting on its perch,
my dazzling pet bird
jingles its glittering chains
 in raucous laughter
to itself,
and sheds its feathers
 in empty space.

(translated from Bengali by Sunil B. Ray and Carolyne Wright with the author)

IMTIAZ DHARKER

PURDAH I

One day they said
she was old enough to learn some shame.
She found it came quite naturally.

Purdah is a kind of safety.
The body finds a place to hide.
The cloth fans out against the skin
much like the earth that falls
on coffins after they put the dead men in.

People she has known
stand up, sit down as they have always done.
But they make different angles
in the light, their eyes aslant,
a little sly.

She half-remembers things
from someone else's life,
perhaps from yours, or mine—
carefully carrying what we do not own:
between the thighs, a sense of sin.

We sit still, letting the cloth grow
a little closer to our skin.
A light filters inward
through our bodies' walls.
Voices speak inside us,
echoing in the spaces we have just left.

She stands outside herself,
sometimes in all four corners of a room.
Wherever she goes, she is always
inching past herself,
as if she were a clod of earth,
and the roots as well,
scratching for a hold
between the first and second rib.

In Their Own Voice

Passing constantly out of her own hands
into the corner of someone else's eyes . . .
while doors keep opening
inward and again
inward.

GRACE

It is not often
that you come across a place
where you are sure to find
some kind of peace.
The masjid at least, you think.
The grace of light through marble,
a space where fear is filtered out.
Perhaps a patch of ground
where you can at last lay down
your own name, and take another on
a bright mantle
that will fold itself around you:
God the Compassionate, the Merciful.

A wash of marble at your feet.
The man at the door turns
to speak. You look for wisdom,
thinking that is what old men are for.
He does not look at you.
Instead, 'A woman comes
with her eyes concealed.
She trails the month behind her.
We are defiled.'

He rolls his reason on his tongue
and spits it out.
You know again the drought
the blazing eye of faith
can bring about.

'Allah-u-Akbar.'
You say the words to reassure yourself.

In Their Own Voice

Your mouth clears.
God the Compassionate, the Merciful,
created man from clots of blood.

'Bismillah.'
You taste it on your tongue.
Salt, sweet.

A clearing in the heart.

ARUNA DHERE

NIGHT HAS COME TO AN END

Night has come to an end, the woman starts her grinding.
Chants her kohl-darkened, sleep-filled couplet to the grindstone
>god.

Round and round go her arms, down pours the flour.
Silent grief across her lap, quietly sucking its fist.

Whatever feelings she may have, those sweepings she brushes
>aside.
The woman empties her mind for the sake of home and hearth.

One ahead, one behind, birth summons her.
The day ends, denying all of this, the day ends.

At dusk, her hand balancing the waterpot, the mother.
Bears the burden of children and menfolk on her head.

One waterpot, one *dudi* above the other, the woman comes
>towards the water.
Not towards the water, but comes to her childhood home.

The water gently sways, the dream enters the water, drowns.
When the moon enters the song, every day she asks for death,
>The woman asks for death.

(translated from Marathi by Asha Mundlay and Arlene Zide)

ASHWINI DHONGDE

SMALL ADS

MATRIMONIALS

Wanted A Bride—Height 5 ft $3\frac{1}{2}$"
>Age—$21\frac{1}{2}$ years
>Very fair, delicate
>Good-looking, slim
>Highly educated graduate, working woman
>(handing over all money to the husband)
>Gentle and submissive
>(able to live under her mother-in-law's thumb)
>Highborn, from a well-to-do family,
>(able to provide an excellent dowry and suitable gifts)
>Hard-working and modest
>Able to adjust to a joint family, no foolish ideas
>(the wind of 'women's lib' not having gone to her head)

Advertising only for a better choice.

Wanted A Groom—No conditions.
>(must be male)
>Adult, either
>Marrying for the first time or
>A widower with children,   anyone will do.

(translated from Marathi by Asha Mundlay and Arlene Zide)

SAROOP DHRUV

PRINCESS DESIRE

Princess Desire!
Still the same,
to and fro in this wilderness—
how long will you go on
living like this?
Or else let me say
that instead of building a nest
you've grown accustomed
to building flimsy webs
and then leaping away?
So far
you've destroyed everything
that has come your way,
whatever has reached your grasp
you've crumbled into a fine powder
and blown away
and then
in the destructive Ganga the dear one bows
repeating the same syllable over and over again.
Still, the itching in your palm doesn't stop?

Now you understand
that the clock's hands
never show twenty-four hours,
but two times twelve they surely strike!
But forgetting even that
you've put on your fancy skirt
and continue dancing away!

Look at me—
the crowds are locusts.
They simply turned into D.D.T.
and flew away, a long time back . . . .
while clapping hands they break apart,
with that raft do you want
to float over to the other end?
Now untie the bells from your ankles . . .

In Their Own Voice

look up
do you see grapes ... hanging anywhere?

Princess Desire!
Have you forgotten that paper tastes
sour-sweet-yellowish-strong!
then go on, jump
and tell me
Yes, yes, speak—should I suck on this, chew this slowly,
                          turn it into pulp and digest it
this paper—this paper in which
there might be maps of palaces or prisons—
there might be fingerprints of red kum kum
                    or blood-wet stains—
there might be anything!
But this shore or that shore!

Do whatever you want, but do something now!
If you can't untie the bells
from your ankles
then finally, do let go of the tambourine—
Do whatever you want, but do something now!
At least
if tonight you can't sleep
then from your collection of poems
tear out a page, roll it into a ball, a pill
put it in your mouth, roll it around
                from side to side, let it melt
and then it becomes—
the dear one bathing
in the destructive Ganga . . . . . .

                              (translated from Gujarati by Sujata Bhatt)

In Their Own Voice

I ASK—'WHY?'*

The son's beloved, the daughter's not,
    I ask, why, I'm asking you, why?
For centuries shall we keep these divisions,
    shall we remain the same? Why? Remain the same.
                      ...Why? I ask.

There was a time when the newborn daughter
died while drinking milk,
but nowadays she's killed off
    in her mother's womb
long before she's due.
                      ...Why? I ask.

When a son is born they share rich *pendahs*
    made from heavy cream,
for a daughter's birth there's only
cheap jalebi—
for she's her mother's shame
    her father's burden.
                      ...Why? I ask.

The son plays so many games,
the daughter does the housework.
The son's winnings bring honour
    to the family,
but the daughter leaves for another home.
                      ...Why? I ask.

They call her someone else's wealth, a nest of snakes
    no one dares to touch.

---

* The form of this poem is the *garbo*, a song form to which Gujarati women do traditional group-dancing. This particular *garbo*/poem has become very popular and well-known, and a number of verses have been added by the women who sing it. Most of the women who sing it are not aware that it is a poem originally written by Saroop Dhruv, and believe it to be another folk *garbo*. The reference to the carriage wheels comes from the folk tradition at the time of marriage when the young couple is told that a bullock cart cannot move without both wheels, that the couple must be truly joined and work together for the marriage to work.

In Their Own Voice

The daughter is a docile cow,
why look after her, they say,
when she'll go wherever you lead her.
                              ...Why? I ask.

They work equally hard, both of them, they work together
but one gets a lot of money, and the other, almost nothing.
                              ...Why? I ask.

The man and the woman, call them two wheels
of the same carriage—if one is high and the other low
then how would the carriage go?
                              ...Why? I ask.

Life is felt equally by all
its joys and sorrows felt equally by all.
But the man enjoys life, and the woman endures all sorrows.
                              ...Why? I ask.

'A son is the light, long live the son,
    and he is the crossbeam supporting the home!'
Saying that, they snatched away
    the daughter's brightness.
                              ...Why? I ask.

The daughter is faint, weak,
and her inner flame struggles
without oil, flickering.
Barely living, how can she sparkle?
How can she eat
the dry left-overs given to her?
                              ...Why? I ask.

The son studies and brings honour to the family
while the daughter does the housework.
No matter how much she learns, she never belongs.
                              ...Why? I ask.

How can she develop only with schooling,
only skilled to read and write?
What more does she have, what bow and arrows
to defend herself

In Their Own Voice

against this hostile fate? Why?

>   I ask: Why?

The stove, the threshold, four walls and the same routine!
Her wings clipped, she's kept in a cage!
A silken net around her! Why?

>   I ask: Why?

From the same orchard, from the same soil,
but the growth is so different, so separate,
as if after planting the seed
one poured poison into the roots!—Why?

>   I ask: Why?

From one blossom there grows a flower,
and soon a garden with many flowers,
Still, in this beautiful world the woman has no part. Why?

>   I ask: Why?

For aeons in this world, the man has always ruled.
Come on friends, colleagues! We'll get together
      and bring equality today,
now we'll bring equality together....
And yet, before that task, there's still other work to be done!
The oppressed, the famished, the unemployed,
      shall we keep them the way they are? Why?
The root of all sorrows, poverty,
      shall we keep it the way it is? Why?
And these walls around caste divisions,
      shall we keep them the way they are? Why?

>   I ask: Why?

(translated from Gujarati by Sujata Bhatt)

CHITRA BANERJEE DIVAKARUNI

MAKING SAMOSAS

We sift salt into chapati flour, pour oil
and skin-warm water. *Punch it
more, more,* my mother says. *The trick
is to get all the kinks out
before you start.* The filling
is already cooling, spread on
the round tin tray on the counter
where this winter day the late sun
catches it briefly, the warm yellow
potatoes, the green glint of peas. She
rolls out the dough that I have made
into little balls, her circles perfect

as in my childhood. *The doctor said
he wasn't to have any,* she says.
*But what rages he would fly into
if we tried to stop him. Remember
that time on your birthday
when he threw the chutney bowl
clear across the room?*
My father, whom we have not seen
these seven years
who hung up each time we called

even after his stroke. I stir
tamarind into the chutney and see him
as she does,
in his kitchen 1500 miles away
his left leg dragging a little.
He peers into the leached white light
of a refrigerator, reaches for
a carton, a bottle. Around him
a city of silent, falling snow.
Stuff carefully, she says, *press too hard
and they'll fall apart.* The oil ready
she slides the samosas in, one by one.

In Their Own Voice

They puff up crisp and golden
hissing.   I lift them
with a slotted spoon and drain them
on newspapers. Her back to me
my mother washes her hands
letting the water run and run. The kitchen
fills with the old brown smell
of roasted cumin, crushed cilantro leaves.

THE BRIDES COME TO YUBA CITY

The sky is hot and yellow, filled
with blue screaming birds. The train
heaved us from its belly
and vanished in shrill smoke.
Now only the tracks
gleam dull in the heavy air,
a ladder to eternity, each receding rung
cleaved from our husbands' ribs.
Mica-flecked, the platform
dazzles, burns up through our thin
chappal soles, lurches
like the ship's dark hold,
blurred months of nights, smell of vomit,
a porthole like the bleached iris
of a giant unseeing eye.

Red-veiled, we lean into each other,
press damp palms, try
broken smiles. Avtar Singh Sodhi,
who met us at the ship, whistles
an *Angrezi* tune
and scans the fields. Behind us,
the black wedding trunks, sharp-edged,
shiny, stenciled with strange men-names
our bodies do not fit into:
Mrs Baldev Johl, Mrs Kanwal Bains.
Inside, folded like wings
bright salwar kameezes scented

In Their Own Voice

with sandalwood. For the men,
kurtas and thin white gauze
to wrap their uncut hair.
Laddus from Jullundhar, sugar-crusted,
six kinds of lentils, a small bag
of bajra flour. Labeled in our mothers'
hesitant hands, pickled mango and lime,
packets of seeds—*methi, karela, saag*
to burst from this new soil
like green stars.

Avtar Singh gives a shout, waves
at the men, their slow
uneven approach. We crease our eyes
through the veils' red film,
cannot breathe. Thirty years
since we saw them. Or never,
like Harvinder, married last year
at Hoshiarpur to her husband's photo,
which she clutches tight to her
to stop the shaking. He is fifty-two,
she is sixteen. Tonight—like us all—
she will open her legs to him.

The platform is endless-wide.
The men walk and walk
without advancing. Their lined,
wavering mouths, their
eyes like drowning lights.
We cannot recognize a single face.

Note: Yuba City, settled by Punjabi farmers around 1910, is now a thriving Indian community in Northern California. Until the 1940s, the Alien Land Laws largely precluded non-white immigrants from owning land, while immigration restrictions prevented their families from joining them.

CHARMAYNE D'SOUZA

MISS-BEGOTTEN

There must have been
some woman in the lineage
who introspected, harvested rice,
bore a son, bored her husband,
and waited till I thought of her—
hawking time like some peddler
with a few well-chosen goods.

History would have been
closer to her than me
(pompous remark, that).
She could have gawked
at St. Francis Xavier (original)
skin, bone and toe intact,
and decided promptly
to eat bread and wine
for the rest of her life,
for the rest of *my* life
for that matter!

Her husband, twirling
his switch-blade Konkan moustache,
may have said—'silly wife!
Now who will marry our daughters?'

Little realizing
that four hundred years later,
his words would ring as true
as the cathedral bells . . .

A good Catholic husband
is still hard to find.

KETAKI KUSHARI DYSON

AFTER READING NAWAL EL SAADAWI'S BOOK
THE HIDDEN FACE OF EVE

Peeling Egyptian potatoes in my kitchen,
I reflect that the
women who helped to grow them
had probably had their clitorises cut off.

In such a world, where we
come to each other so maimed,
fractions, not integers,
less than our whole selves.

what can our laughter,
our articulate loves,
art, science, or
separate lusts achieve?

Clitorises? Tongues? Hair?
Noses? Uteri? Breasts?

The centuries! And all of us connivers!
Words, Silences, Structures we uphold:
those ornate arches
we so love to laud.

I implore you,
all who read my lines,
if you have mothers,
sisters, wives, or daughters,

remember those
who have been forced to pay
in the high-inflated currency of pain
for being born women.

And should a woman
dare to speak out loud

In Their Own Voice

about how she has been
mauled by love or hate,

suffer her to speak.
Do not shut her up.

PIA GANGULY

CHOICES OF A KING'S MISTRESS

with Tuglaq's morning cup of coffee
came news that his mistress had died
turning over his newspaper
to the financial page, he said
it's God's grace, i was
bored with her anyway

ABOUT THE LADY WHO BUYS A PINT OF VODKA TWICE A DAY

when Mona Lisa had a moustache
it was her
and the agony of having
to be the man of the family
drove her to it

PRABHA GANORKAR

LANGUAGE

Nowadays when people talk to me
or even to each other,
it's only through thick
soundproof glass.
Only lips move
in blank faces.
Or I move among them
as in a foreign country:
Without dialogue.
I have lost the meaning
of tongues.
Books black on white
invitations in gold
mere squiggles without
intent
for language is not a context
of life.

Such as touch:
but that too has lost its soul
and is no more than
a sponge swabbing a table,
without the contexts of tenderness:
Mother's fingers through hair
Father's pat on the back;
these have almost vanished.

Other words are almost obscene
conventions of social usage
the sentence of the night
is one, blunted, worn-smooth.
Nowadays, we don't use the eyes
To convey the heart.
They do, who want to eye
The words,
Unpronounceable by the tongue.

In Their Own Voice

It becomes almost impossible
To live
Without language.

So I find for myself
a language that makes
such numbness endurable.
I listen to: trembling leaves
rustling breeze
opening petals
hissing raindrops on
parched earth.
It is well that I understand
this
language.

(translated from Marathi by Gauri Deshpande)

GAGAN GILL

SHE WILL COME BACK IN HER BODY

She will desire him like sin
She will desire him like virtue

In some unknown place
In an unknown room
She will make love to him in her thoughts

As though, for no reason
Uninvited, she has gone there
Walking in her sleep
As though for centuries she's been sitting
At that place within herself
Where nightmares lie in wait
For desires to go mad.

She will desire him
Like a kind of dream
That, only with open eyes
She has always seen
As though he were a shoulder
For some barren cry.

As though loving were a curse
Were an endless wailing
Or an incoherent monologue
She will desire him.

As though desire protected you from happiness
And was a defence against sorrow
She will desire him.

As though he
Were some incurable disease
As though he were
Something to be lifted
Like a sorcerer's spell
She will desire him.
She will desire him

In Their Own Voice

Like sin
She will desire him like virtue
And come back in her body

Like a hidden wound.

(translated from Hindi by Mrinal Pande and Arlene Zide)

THE FIFTH MAN

Moving towards the hangman's noose
The fifth man steps
Onto the fifth place
Whether it is daylight or dark, the fifth man watches
His own shadow
On the fifth place
Only the fifth man believes
That there are four ahead of him

Till the very end he believes
That he will not be the fifth.

(translated from Hindi by Mrinal Pande and Arlene Zide)

PADMA GOLE

THE DREAD OF MOTHERHOOD

Never until now was I so afraid to be a mother.
Never have I felt so sad, so bitter with the sense of helplessness.
You asked me today:
>Which path do I choose?
My very lifesbreath rises in my throat,
Eyes fill to overflowing
Which direction do I point out to you?
East? West? North? South?
This dread that has frozen me, has also turned the four of them
>>to stone!

Where is knowledge? Success? Happiness?
What are the signs to know them by?
Whichever way you look you find the devil, in one guise or another.
The atom bomb pervades—land, water, even the sky
Every path is drenched in human blood.
Not even a mother's breast can offer shelter to a child today.
Like the missile of the son of Drona*
The blast from Hiroshima strikes.
Where can you go? You have to go somewhere.
You must.
No one, however, shows you how.

Child, don't lose courage
Keep on looking; find your own path
Take any direction, but whichever way you take, keep your
>>humanity.
Have courage, put your foot forward, run now
No time to lose,
Just remember one thing—everyone has a mother.

---

* Drona's son, Ashwatthama, is a character in the *Mahabharata* who, against all the etiquette of war, came stealthily at night to kill Draupadi's five sleeping infant sons.

(translated from Marathi by Ashok Kelkar, Asha Mundlay and Arlene Zide)

In Their Own Voice

THERE'S STILL SOMETHING LEFT

On the road or by the river's edge
or, suddenly, in a private moment
even now, when our eyes chance to meet
they glance away.
There's still something left.

Even now, when we exchange a few polite words
unknowingly, nectar drips
from them, relieves the pain in my breast.
There's still something left.

Both of us feign indifference
but our hearts hope for something else.
We loose an arrow
hoping it will rebound.
We keep the wound bleeding.

(translated from Marathi by Asha Mundlay and Arlene Zide)

TEJI GROVER

SONG OF SEPARATION

I'm writing like this
As if meeting my blind children
In an orphanage, many years later.

How tall they've grown
Since you left

How small the words
I brought to clothe them in!

Often,
Some friend or other
He'll say to me

>   (How can he say that
>   If he's a true friend?)—

>   Come on, fall in love
>   Again, *yar*!
>   Look, just because
>   This guy crossed over the bridge,
>   Doesn't mean you have
>   To burn down the whole bridge after him!

I say:

>   Which bridge?
>   Which guy?
>   Are you in your right senses,
>   my love?
>   Just watch,

And suddenly,
Faster than flame streaks along a dry straw
I want to run away.
Desires run faster than I do
In this fleeing body.
Surely, this is the emptiness of the body
Which moves ahead of me,

In Their Own Voice

Makes a fire,
Sits itself down.
In the fire
That guy who crossed the bridge
Is not there

Not there—
His shadow
Stands still
In the water below the bridge.

No
Even the bridge is not there

So tell me, man
Where am I standing
And what am I saying?

(translated from Hindi by Aruna Sitesh and Arlene Zide)

KAMALA HEMMIGE

DO YOU KNOW?

You who grow cactii
In flowerpots, and wear
Roses in your hair
Do you know
about the nude women
Worshipping their god
In Chandragutthi?

You aesthetes who wear
necklaces of your new freedom
Do you know
that a pearl can buy a girl
in Savadatthi?

You respectable ones
Who've never been in court
Do you know
Rapists are acquitted
And the dishonoured
Auctioned off?

You skilful ones
Who can drink tea
Without smudging your lipstick
Do you know
the story of the girl
who was stripped naked
for wanting to eat?

(translated from Kannada by Tejaswini Niranjana)

POPATI HIRANANDANI

A RARE TREASURE

Your eyes glide down, below the navel,
Ah! Is it a glowing treasure-house?
Or a deep mysterious cave
Where the stream of creation flows?

Is it the delicate bit of Eve's tenderness
Or the entrance to the world for Man?
It may look like an elephant's face
but it is easily pierced by the arrow of your heart.

Some feel it is the heart of woman
The goal of the deepest desires of men
Is it the labyrinth where only lust lingers
Or the storehouse for all of women's misery?

It is woman's strength, her weakness too
The stunning game of Purush-Prakriti, nature and universal man.
It's true, they call it The Engulfing One,
For it devours his pride, his personality, his name.

It ripens, brightens the great human seed
The preserver of the entire human race
And yet in its pursuit, the cause of all struggle, every strife
The source of all humanity's abuse.

The rhythm of happiness,
The intoxication of pleasure, it is an illusion
Of the union of man and woman,
The aid to reaching the fourfold goal of existence of man.

The beauty in all the arts, the game of politics,
Experiments spiritual or mundane
All encircling go round this treasure so rare
As man dances around it again and again.

(translated from Sindhi by the author with editing by Arlene Zide)

IVARA
(V. INDIRA BHAVANI)

AVATARS

when he reads
smutty books
that foul the waters
a contagion
in the depths of society
and smacks his lips over them
in his own room
all alone

                      he's the Fish

when he shrinks within his own shell
and hides himself
as others call upon him
to do good, strong deeds

                      he's the Tortoise

when he falls flat on his face
in an ocean of booze
and eagerly creates
a singular sort of world

                      he's the Pig

at the office
when he makes the workers dance
and claws the files
    the men
    their work
    to tatters

                      he's Narasimha the Man-lion

when wishes for undercover bribes
sprout up
and molder
spore by spore
in a heart full of cobwebs

                              he's the Dwarf

when he roots out
people he doesn't like
as he bears his hoe-weapon
in his bent heart

                              he's Rama-with-the-axe

when he takes
loud oaths
of monogamy
in bed
and says
> Dear
> I'll never touch
> anyone else
> in this life
> not even in my heart

                              he's Lord Rama

when he hides himself
behind dark glasses
enjoying women
fore and aft
on buses and off
and takes special pleasure
in two separate houses
in faraway places

                              he's Lord Kṛṣṇa

In Their Own Voice

and so on and so forth
if you look more deeply
inside this man
you will see
even a thousand avatars there
>stand aside:
>he's no less than
>an avatar himself

(translated from Tamil by Martha Ann Selby and K. Paramasivam)

SUNITA JAIN

WHAT IS IT

Looking at her, I keep wondering
on which peg
she hangs her dreams
I know
she hasn't
set her heart on anyone yet.
Out of terror of her father
or her mother's hawklike eye?

Even so
there must be something
she applies like kohl, tempering her loneliness.

She's my daughter
half my age
And when even younger than she
travelling, I would often tell myself
looking at a straw hut, or a mango grove:
If the person that I loved
was living here
then I would live here too.
He would go to work
And I would wait there cooking.
I dreamed my innocent dreams,
smaller than sparrows,
but like a rocket, life took off.
It's not a hut, but a spacious house
where the food is placed on the table
and no one waits for anyone —
only sometimes I

catch my tender young daughter,
her eyes as fresh as an untouched *diya* lamp,
smiling to herself
and I wonder:

In Their Own Voice

Nothing of her
is hidden from me
But what is it
which even she
is unaware of?

(translated from Hindi by Aruna Sitesh and Arlene Zide)

NAYANA JANI

THE SOUNDLESS EXPLOSION

Something breaks and cracks, merges with something else
Whatever once was made of gold, again melts into a lump of
                                                                            gold.
The mountains are submerged, the oceans surge
Then azure sky turns wet and crouches down in showers.
Nothing can be found where it once was.
All forts and castles come crashing down in this upheaval.
Even that which was collected and preserved for endless births
                                                                            melts, loses shape.
Existence itself dissolves into an elixir.
In the soundless explosion of this moment
Only those who without ears can listen, hear it.

               (translated from Gujarati by the author and edited by Arlene Zide
                                                                             and Bharat Pathak)

JAYA PRABHA

LOOKS

Looks
From two eyes
Dart like needles
Roam freely on flesh.

The looks never
Look into the face
The words never come from the heart
They crawl on the body
Like white ants
Disgust every time I see them.

Those eyes
Belong to a million classes
But their looks are all the same.

Only one signal
In those looks
Hunger like a salivating dog's
An ugly bear-fist
Chases you even in dreams
No difference between day and night
In this thick forest
No place at all
To escape these looks

On the road
In buses, classrooms

Behind your every step
Wounding
Some part of the body
Looks tipped with poison
Keep pricking you

Frightened
I want to disappear
Into the distant sky, into emptiness

In Their Own Voice

But
Escape is no solution
So I began to teach my eyes
The sharpness of thorns
To fight those poison looks

Now to chase away those eyes
I fight with my eyes
Timid eyes which
Cannot look straight
For two seconds,
Run to the underworld

A day will come
When women in this country have
Thorns
Not only in their eyes
But all over their bodies.

(translated from Telugu by Velcheru Narayana Rao and A. K. Ramanujan)

BHAGYA JAYASUDARSHANA

FOR AKKA*

You cut all the knots that
Bound you and became
Free of the constraints
Imposed from within and without.
You were bold, firmly resolved
In your outbursts and silences.

The clothes with which you draped your soul
Turned greener in your inner storms
Your thunders and rains,
Your enemies surrendered to you
In the battle you had waged
In the open fields of elemental
Movements, you were the empress
Of the empire of Channa Mallikarjuna.

In the battles which I fight, I hold
The weapons, weapons that
Cannot rust, weapons
That cannot be sharpened, weapons
Of mud and plaster;
I roam in the circle of my defeats.
Oh, I haven't gone naked, roaming
The streets of small desires.
But, *Akka* do you know
My nakedness within,
And that I've shivered
With the winter's cold.

---

* the well-known twelfth century woman poet and seer of Karnataka, Akka Mahadevi

(translated from Kannada by the author)

MAMTA KALIA

MARITAL BLISS

Eight years after marriage
When first I came back home
Mom and daddy asked
'Are you happy? Tell the truth.'

I should have just laughed off
Such a useless question,
But I started crying;
Between sobs, nodded
Neither yes nor no.
I wanted to tell them
I was happy on Tuesday,
Sad on Wednesday. That
One day I'd be laughing at 8 o'clock
And crying at quarter past.

I wanted to tell them
How one day
We finished off a whole watermelon
And were all happy.
How once I cried the whole night
Pushing away thoughts of suicide
Somehow.
That in a family of fourteen
It's a struggle to stay happy.

But mom and daddy
Sat there looking at my sons
Running about wildly
Like chubby little goats.
Mom and daddy's wrinkled faces,
Eyelids and hands
Trembling.
I swallowed everything
And smiled like a contented woman.

(translated from Hindi by Aruna Sitesh and Arlene Zide)

M. R. KAMALA

DREAMS ON SALE

Once a year
When some festival is in the offing
The millers at Garden*
Stick discount labels
On torn-off old saris
and keep dreams for sale.

They build a fairy land
In the hearts of middle class women.

When you enter this 'garden'
You see
Flowers of different kinds and colours
Blue sky
Silvery cloud
Star-like stickers
Flowing waters
Roaring waterfalls
They stick illusory wings
On every wonder of nature.

Damsels
Letting down
Their sari pleats
Girls
In tight *churidar* pants
TV announcers
The intellectuals of Kalakshetra
—all embrace these heaps of saris
Wonder-eyed

They let themselves
Bathe
In the ocean of colours

---

* the textile company

In Their Own Voice

Rise and float
Despite the blazing sun
The flowing sweat.

They pour out the money
They collected all year
and
Buy their dreams

Surpassing even triumphant emperors
Their eyes become
Stars
Batteries of lightning
Reflecting the fulfilment
Of their lives.

(translated from Kannada by Sandhya S.)

LAKSHMI KANNAN

DRAUPADI

Once more
stripped to the raw nerves
the bones vibrating cold,
Draupadi is bared in books
papers, case-studies,
written about, explained, clinically justified
peeled of mythical euphemism
that covered her physiognomy, anatomy, her psyche,
discussed till she is wrung out dry—
a subject.

Eased of the weight
of an anachronistic civilization
which once bent her double,
She has now straightened up to stand easy,
looks clear as sheer glass
through which you see everything.
The global features on her face
launched a thousand UN meetings
and a conference at Copenhagen.
The garments She is now offered
to wrap herself for warmth
are resolutions on thin paper.

The pain was more tangible years ago
when She was a mere palpitating organism
beaten and kicked about.
The swollen blue and purple bruises
on her body
won her quick, straight sympathy
Not beaten anymore
Draupadi stands bare of bruises
her heart arrested at a still point in history.

She has done it.
Has offended the supreme male
into a sullen silence
by her terrible nakedness

MANJU KAPUR

BIRDS

In my dream
Women flew
Larger than any
Birds I had seen.

They flew high
They flew together
Over trees
And dry, dusty land.

They came back, some
After years, with water
Careful in their beaks
For those who had
Forgotten how to fly.

KETU KATRAK

MEMORIES OF EXILE

I

I become an expert
at tight-rope walking.
Spanning oceans
a balancing act.
'Don't forget where you come from,'
a whisper in the blood.
I keep the American dream at bay.
My soul slinks
between the screen door
and the glass door
looking for a space
to belong.

II

In stillness
my mind travels
under the wheels
of the speeding train
seeking
the still centre
of the spinning-wheel.
The rhythm replays,
'speeding to a non-destination,
speeding to a new non-belonging'
curious destiny
of ex-
patriates,
of the lost people
clamouring like ants
not welcome
on the outer crust
of the apple-pie

Third-worlders
thrice-removed from
their center.

III

A refrain echoes
after each plunge
into the abyss
of unlearning
from experience:
'A pattern. In relationships.'

> Don't tell me about history.
> It doesn't repeat.
> Only each seeming repetition
> begins and ends
> at a new point.
> We struggle to wrench meaning
> out of each echo
> if we can hear ourselves.

Sometimes
I reach a space
between day and night
conflictual light
echoing
a desire to remain
within the arc of your arm
and discover the bitter knowledge
of not belonging
not to this space,
not to myself.

KATYAYANI

CHAMPA, AMONG SEVEN BROTHERS

Graceful as a reed,
Champa grew to womanhood
Among seven brothers.
But like a snake she writhed upon her father's chest.
She would wander, a black shadow
In his dreams.
Champa grew to womanhood
Among seven brothers.

> She got pounded
> In the mortar with the paddy
> And thrown upon the trash heap
> With the husks.
> There like the *Amarbel** vine
> She grew
> And came back in the house.

One day the Champa who'd grown to womanhood with seven
  brothers
Was discovered
Hanging from the roof
And was buried deep among the nets of weeds within the pond.
There, rising from the net,
A blue lotus bloomed.
Champa came back into the house,
Was offered to the Gods,
Was crushed when she had wilted, and then thrown away
Was burnt
Her ashes scattered
Through the village.

At night it poured and poured
The very next day

Outside every door
Sat the fearless, untouched Champa

---
* a parasitic creeper or vine

In the middle of the thorny cactus bushes
Smiling.

(translated from Hindi by Mrinal Pande and Arlene Zide)

THE LUMP OF JAGGERY

He throws tantrums
The child howls and stamps his feet
For a lump of jaggery.
The mother says there isn't any
Yet the child is unshakeable in his obstinacy
He knows
Somewhere in a knot at the end of her sari
Or in some corner of her wicker basket
Mother must have hidden
A little lump of jaggery just for him
Away from the eyes of the world.
Even if Creation comes to an end
Or the whole world is turned upside down
That lump will be safe
Under the edge of his mother's sari
Among seven layers
No emperor can grab it
No ghosts or evil spirits make it disappear.

Indra, the rain-god
Cannot melt it in the rain
Mother will render everyone impotent
With her power.
Even if that lump of jaggery is lost
In the field, or the storehouse, or the tea gardens
Or In the stone-quarry,
Wherever
Mother will hunt for it from one end of the universe to the other

And rediscover it for her little darling.
The child howls

In Their Own Voice

For the little lump of jaggery
That mother has hidden away just for him
With all due precaution
Somewhere.

(translated from Hindi by Mrinal Pande and Arlene Zide)

N. KRISHNA KUMARI

CARBON DIOXIDE

I am carbon dioxide
The redness just visible
Between man and man,
Flames in the recesses of conscience
I extinguish.
Flashes of brow-knittings,
Half-mad unconcern I know.
The ugly misshapen curve of ridicule
Flashing in the curl of a lip
I remember.
In the creases of conscience
In the dirt-ridden folds,
On the erupting flames of disgust
I rain ferociously.
I dance the dance of annihilation.
It is just the very same tale
Behind all flames
The tale that fosters jealousy
Like a demon between man and man
The dirty tale
Is the very same for all creation.
The strange tale of thought
Like doors barred
Between heart and heart
Is the same everywhere.
It smolders, spewing sparks.
Where it gathers easily into flame
Humanity becoming ashes
Is the glee of inhumanity.
The five-hued parrot
What does it matter what name you call it by
Tongue-biting and blister-raising
Lime water I would transform
Into a pure milky liquid.
I am carbon dioxide

In Their Own Voice

Heiress
To the callous spouting mad wind
I will extinguish flames
Rising madly between man and man,
Cool the kindling blaze.

(translated from Telugu by V. V. B. Rama Rao)

KAMAL KUMAR

NEW GENERATION

He —
sticks the poster
of his freedom
on my forehead.
Shouts slogans
demanding his rights,
Splits my eardrums
with his loud voice.

Declares his new vision
by poking
his fingers in my eyes.
Hands me the verdict
on his birth and circumstances,
setting the whip
of ethics and new values
to my back.

Pushes aside
his heritage
like some broken potsherd.
Lighting brand-new sparklers,
puts out the light.

There, teetering on one leg,
stretching his hand into the wind
to touch the new sky of the new century
is my young son,
representative
of the new generation.

(translated from Hindi by Aruna Sitesh and Arlene Zide)

KUSUM

from I WANTED TO HAVE A DAUGHTER

I wanted to have a daughter
so that I could learn
that my heart doesn't break for a girl.
If my son falls, gets a fever, feels pain,
or grows angry, I know
that my heart breaks, my mind is thrown into turmoil.
(For him I'd even burn my daughter-in-law.)
But how is it possible
that this won't happen for a daughter?
I was born a girl, so my parents didn't really want me,
they say they kept me for practical reasons.
Would they have really done so?
Kept me to do chores, to look after my younger brother,
to earn themselves the merit
of making the gift of a virgin daughter,
or to get a man as a son-in-law?
My husband and his family didn't want me,
so why did he marry me?
For a servant-girl at his beck and call,
a mental slave, a cushion to sleep on,
a womb to produce a child, a doll to put on show,
or a promissory note for a dowry?
Barter away one woman, then breed and get another one.
Did he really marry *me*?
If I'd had a daughter, I would have
screamed at her, neglected her, put her to work,
drowned her in milk, fed her opium,
used her for wood in the stove,
turned her into a temple-dancer, a common musician,
or even a whore, sold her, buried her,
starved her, branded her,

sent her off as quickly as possible to her in-laws,
and on top of it all taught her
to commit sati.

My heart wouldn't have broken for her,
my mind wouldn't have been broken into turmoil.
Really, it wouldn't have broken for her....

(translated from Marathi by Vinay Dharwadker)

APABRITA LAHIRI

FIRSTNESS

Two dogs bark. Before the barking were the many sounds of our words. After, only quiet. Again that barking... it stops in a while. Now perhaps the dogs are barking again. Perhaps there are no sounds in that field. We came away—did that quietness come with us? Then there must be a deep peace reigning over the field, as when we were talking.

(translated from Bengali by Chitra Banerjee Divakaruni)

PERMISSION

Give me back my work with all its weight. It will take me a long time to be able to say this. After many days, perhaps. I will join my palms, I will look at the sun, I will say, *give me back my work with all its weight.* I will say this when the sun is rising from the east, or perhaps sinking into the west. For you cannot pray to the midday sun.

(translated from Bengali by Chitra Banerjee Divakaruni)

CHITRA LAHIRI

RAVAGED BLOSSOM

Ravaged blossom, woman alone
        Cover your face.
The terraced grainfields are strewn with the feathers of
                              hummingbirds.
The finger-cymbals' last faint notes have sounded
In the bloodied vagina of the Maharani.
Now, in the inviting scent of the wind
There are no dreams.
The last ferry has drifted away,
The flow of fine words damped.
Drenched, your address has run in the drizzling rain.

Woman alone,
Within the mountain, burn your soul.
Lift your face to the glow of the bridal sunset-light.
The cloud that bends low
Over the leaf-sheltered shade of the forest
Is not yours.
Part of the West Wind has been stolen.
In the embryo
Scatter what is left.

                (translated from Bengali by Paramita Banerjee and Arlene Zide)

JYOTI LANJEWAR

I NEVER SAW YOU

Ma
I never ever saw you
in a brand new silk *Eerakal* sari
bordered in gold
a necklace of gold coins
at your throat
Bangles and bracelets on your wrists
Wearing rubber chappals on your feet
Ma
I saw you . . .
Fixing the roads
in a work gang
Your bare feet burning
on the burning ground
Your kid in some cloth
slung on the thorny branches of the babul tree
while you carried the vats of tar
I saw you . . .
Baskets of earth on your head
Your feet wrapped in rags and leaves
I saw you kiss your naked child
who ran to you
on pattering feet
while you slaved
for your daily wage.
I saw you . . .
Help to build the lake dam
Dragging a chain of tears behind you
Kneading the gut of your belly
while, tormented by thirst
your own lips went parched
I saw you . . .
Gingerly placing your pregnancy-swollen feet
as you climbed the bamboo scaffolding
high on a beautiful new house

In Their Own Voice

Carrying loads
of cement and sand on your head
Wanting
even a four-walled shelter of your own
I saw you . . .
Late in the evening
infant at your breast
Untying the little bundle knotted in the end of your sari
Buying a little oil and salt
Saving a small shiny coin
to put in my tiny palm
Saying:
    Get yourself something to eat
Saying:
    Get yourself an education like Ambedkar
    And me done with toting baskets!
I saw you . . .
Burning the sticks of your body
Lighting a stack
of dry sugarcane for fuel
in the stove
Feeding everyone else
on four coarse *bhakris**
Half-starving yourself
Saving a small piece in your sari
for later.
I saw you . . .
Washing clothes, scrubbing pots and pans
in four different houses
But keeping your dignity
Refusing
to take leftovers
Modestly covering yourself
with the same end of
your rag of a seven-times-knotted sari
in which you made your countless little bundles

---

* bhakri: coarse, round, unleavened bread

In Their Own Voice

I saw you . . .
Right in the middle of the town-square
cursing out
the mother and sister of any man
who dared to look at you with lecherous eyes
I saw you . . .
Bearing heavy baskets of fruit through the crowds
drawing the end of your sari over your head
when someone dared to bump into you
Threatening
him with your raised chappal
I saw you . . .
after lifting and carrying
a mountain of work
at the end of the day
I saw
Your feet turn homeward
slicing the darkness
angrily throwing out your man
who had come back drunk
I saw you . . .
on the Long March*
striding out in front
sari drawn tight around you
Shouting:
    We must change our name
Enduring the crack
of a police club on your arm
Going to jail
with your head held high
I saw you . . .
Saying to your only son,

---

* the Long March took place in Maharashtra in 1956 and was organized by the followers of Dr B. R. Ambedkar ('Babasaheb'). It was part of the movement which resulted in the mass-conversion of about three million Maharashtrian untouchables to Buddhism. After the event, the converts adopted the label 'Dalit' meaning 'ground down, oppressed'.

In Their Own Voice

martyred in a police shooting:
>You died for Bhima
>Your life gained meaning

Defiantly telling the policeman
that if you'd had two or three sons
you'd have been more fortunate
you'd have fought again
I saw you...
on your deathbed cot
counting your last moments
with a gift to charity
Of the money you'd made and saved
sifting through papers and trash
I saw you...
Saying:
>Live in unity
>Fight for Babasaheb
>Build him a memorial

Breathing your last with the words
*Jai Bhima** on your lips
I never saw you
praying at your beads
for a brand new silk *Eerakal* sari
Ma
I saw you...

---

* Bhima refers to Dr Ambedkar as well as to the character in the *Mahabharata*, who was physically the strongest and most heroic of the five Pandavas. Bhima is thus a ubiquitous double symbol of power, strength, resilience, tenacity, and heroic struggle in Dalit writing. 'Jai Bhima' means 'Victory to Bhima'.

(*translated from Marathi by Tilottama Daswani and edited by Vinay Dharwadkar and Arlene Zide with additional stanzas translated by Vinay Dharwadkar*)

JOYSHREE LOBO

THE JACKALS WAIT BELOW

I met him half a century ago —
He sat astride the roof
Of a train to Pakistan.
He spouted religious purity,
The rules of democracy,
And later under cover of
Soothing darkness,
Complacent, drugged sleep —
He slit throats, chopped limbs —
Feeding morsels to the dogs below.

He looked younger, ruddy-cheeked
More bloated,
On the streets of Nellie,
In the fields of Mongoldai.
He added arson and loot
To his armoury.
The cries of children,
Outraged, bleeding women,
Broken limbed men —
Were music to his ears.

Last night he sat
By a sacred fire, performing holy rites,
Adding incense, flowers,
Butter and sandalwood,
To create a fragrant smokescreen,
As he bowed before a brick.
He carried it
From home to hearth,
From town to village,
Crashing cymbals,
Blowing trumpets,
Whisking flies
With peacock feathers.

In Their Own Voice

In his wake he leaves
Blood tears and gore,
Broken vessels, shattered lives,
Crushed bangles,
Smeared sindoor—
While the jackals wait below.

PRAVASINI MAHAKUD

BEFORE ANYONE COMES

Before anyone comes, I will return
As the daybreak, as a garland of dewdrops,
To morning's first step I will come
On gentle feet
Restless with impatience, to the waiting earth.
To light I move from darkness
I want to be the light.

Before anyone comes
I want to be a voice lost
In the chirping of the birds
Wipe the sun's scent from their wings
Drench them
In a bouquet of blessings.
Let's see if, just like that I can beat my wings
I am a lonely bird flying the empty blue skies.
Making no conditions, ready—
I declare my presence.

Before anyone comes
I am willing to be a river,
To quench the thirst of the entire world
Willing to be a tiny stream
In fields green with paddy
Where the farmer's whole year of dreams
Is suspended searching the sky.

If another Buddha were to descend,
Releasing a thousand doves of peace
From the cruel hands of a barbarous Ashok,
Proclaiming love from his pitiless heart
In the place of war,
I might become the banks of the river Niranjana,
The shadow of the Bodhi tree.

Before anyone comes,
I am willing to be a torch

In Their Own Voice

If the coming morning's path ahead is brightened
By erasing miles and miles of darkness.
From this time on.
I might become a seedling.
if, some years from now, of even a single wayfarer,
My shadow might ease the weariness.

I might spin a cocoon
Before anyone comes,
And after a few days, become a beautiful butterfly.
If children in a future garden
Ran to catch me on their tiny feet,
Drowning the cackle of birds with their sweet babble.
I might become a kite
To be flown through azure skies.
I might become a flower,
In the garden of time, the whole year long,
Become its pollen, become the fragrance
In its honeyed petals.

Before anyone comes,
I might become a canvas.
There'll come an artist who will paint on me
With all the colours of his heart,
The greatest picture of the 21st century.
Become a mountain of words,
A neverending stream of passion,
For some poet-storyteller who will write
Life's epic.

Before anyone comes,
I might become Mother Mary or Devaki
And give the gift of Jesus and Krishna
To the world.
I might become a sky
Without the threat of star wars
Stronger than a thunderbolt.

In Their Own Voice

For that man suffering in disease and pain,
I might become a honeyed, gentle touch.
Wherever I am,
No matter how far away,
I'll return,
A dream of the future.

(translated from Oriya by J. P. Das and Arlene Zide)

ANURADHA MAHAPATRA

GOD

I have not seen God.
When I see temples I think
of Hiranyakashipu* the demon king,
and when I see an image worshipped
I think about the daughter of the house
being sold for cash. Offering
one faded life to another.
To see blood coughed
from the mouths of the bloodless
is the final joke.
    Still, when I saw that fellow
in the grimy blue-black tee-shirt on the tram,
straight as a cast-iron cannon, I wished he were God!
Then at least I'd have gotten
a proper place to hide,
or I could have pushed him
and even if he'd been killed
I could have loved him.
    Nowadays when I put my foot
on the running board of a bus
I think of God.

---

* usually depicted in temple iconography being torn apart by Narasimha, the lion-headed incarnation of the god Vishnu.

Note: This poem exemplifies, albeit in an extreme and contemporary urban form, the *bhakti* (devotional) tradition of seeing God in all forms of life, even the lowest.

(translated by Jyotirmoy Datta and Carolyne Wright)

In Their Own Voice

BUSINESSWOMAN'S STORY

Sunday goes by in marijuana, but
the village girl's entire year
goes nowhere. The seasons change in stars
and genitals, but this year what she owes
in town are no small debts.
On the border of her white widow's sari*
black sweat drops; the funeral meal,**
worship of the dark-skinned goddess,
and the half-burnt hut set her to wondering,
though in her body countless seeds
give off their ripe aroma.
The child in the marijuana shop
rocking on his broken ribs
is the flower of her lap,
the harvest month's granary. In fact,
carrying all of death's addictions
in her belly-cloth at night,
dozing on a half-burnt mat
in her half-demolished hut all year,
she grows old in the receding hopes of business.

---

* the white widow's sari is actually, in Bengali, the *dhuti* (dhoti), the husband's garment, worn as a widow's sari after his death.

** the 'funeral meal' is the *habishya*, a sacrificial meal of boiled rice and ghee eaten during ceremonies including funerals. It is the widow's first meal after the cremation of her husband.

Note: In certain villages, widows left with no inheritance or means of earning a living must often resort to prostitution or small-scale smuggling of liquor, foodstuffs or drugs in order to feed themselves and their children.

(translated by Paramita Banerjee and Carolyne Wright)

UMA MAHESWARI

OF MY OWN

The smudgy mosaic
of the kitchen
the soot of the vessels
in my fingernails
the washing line
fluttering in the breeze
have usurped the dreams
I dreamt once.
Now it's a way of life.

But then
the business of camouflaging pain
under a cheerful facade
comes naturally to me.
Analysing myself egotistically,
I compared myself with others
only to increase the agony.

The moon wails from a far-off distance
the sheep graze in the fields
unquestioningly.
The heart weighs heavy
as conversation echoes
with the emptiness of conch shells
in a funeral march.
I escape these
to become a broken shell
spat out on the shore
by the sea.

(translated from Tamil by Lakshmi Kannan)

SUJATHA MATHAI

ISHVARI'S VOICE

Ishvari would lie down
on a mat in my room at night.
Unbinding her long hair,
Loosening the folds of her *mundu*,
Shaking out the grass mat,
And sighing, after the long day,
She'd speak to me
Or perhaps, to anyone out there in the night.
She spoke of her lovers,
Of the one who had killed himself,
his beautiful body, with the lights of
        his male desire,
Put out for ever.
Of the boy babies who lay dead—
Lovely fair babies, Amma,
boys left to die by the Hospital Gates—
unwanted babies, illicit desires.
Is desire ever illicit? Are babies ever illegitimate?
Those lovely boy babies, some girls too
Why did they die?
If you touch the raw edge of
        life's jagged surfaces
You get wounded.
Out there it's dark.
The cobra lays eggs
Which ensure another generation.

The retina of the night is unflickering.
Ishvari, domestic servant, has
        known it all.
Abandonment. To be abandoned.
Her eyes—cold and indifferent
        in the daytime
Become phosphorescent at night
        —like a cat's.

SHAKUNT MATHUR

CHILKA LAKE

This is someone's sleep
laid out
like that other world untouched by anyone.
The dream that got drowned here
is awake
in no condition to say anything,
some large boat
capsized within its depths.
That's why this lake
with its large, dark eyes
looks so peaceful.
On all sides, the hills rising;
to the North, the moving boats—
so peaceful.

They say it's an arm of the sea,
but the sea is violent
its deafening roar quickly rising and falling
coiled waves, rolling over
and this lake—
a guesthouse right in the middle
where people come, stare
and go away again,
stunned deer stand around, watching.

Today there's no one here
Outside, inside, eerie silence.
The night is deep
I and you
You and I
Not even me.
Not even us.
Just the depths of this lake
in which a boat has sunk.

(translated from Hindi by Aruna Sitesh and Arlene Zide)

In Their Own Voice

WAITING

Scolded
the old servant
for his usual slowness
Gave a good slap
to my darling son
for his mischief
To my daughter who'd been playing
gave a dozen hankies to hem
Ordered
the oldest one
to drink more milk
Washed
all the dirty clothes
Flipped through a few magazines
Darned some torn clothes
Put on some new buttons
Cleaned the machine and oiled it
Put the cover back on with care
Took out the half-finished sewing
and repacked it in a different way
Wiped the cupboards in the kitchen
Cleaned the spice jars.

And still
he
hasn't come home from the office.

(translated from Hindi by Aruna Sitesh and Arlene Zide)

R. MEENAKSHI

I'LL SING FOR MANKIND

O Ad-man

man of the advertising *yuga*
who hawks things like some merchant
straighten out your bent ears
and listen

there's the professor
who tames our minds
kindles wisdom in us
and points his finger
to the path of experience
and the leaders well-versed in politics
who sound off from their diases
about the responsibility of citizens
write books
and hold elections
then there are those who cure disease
plead court cases
pass judgement
build buildings
sell
buy
why?
there's more
there are those who plow and reap
fall asleep at their looms
beat away with sledgehammers
beget children and rear them
they've all become false
let our creator
do his handiwork

what this town needs
is a pandit-barber
to shave off

127

In Their Own Voice

the prickly bristles
on the face of life

and we need a dhobi of fire
to bleach clean
that heap of humanity
that floats in shit
mixed with swarming sorrows

and to scoop up and bury
all the waste
that blackly settles
both inside and out
what we need right now
is some scavenger of miracles
with a sense of humour

(translated from Tamil by Martha Ann Selby and K. Paramasivam)

O HEROINE OF MADURAI

O Heroine of Madurai,
our Fish-eyed Mother,
when your daughter
climbed the steps
crossed the threshold
circled the tank
saw the parrot on your shoulder
and came running to your side
your very own son
molested her.

Even in the temple
there's no protection.

In your time,
you gorgeous thing,
how did you go out on procession?

(translated from Tamil by Martha Ann Selby and K. Paramasivam)

JAYA MEHTA

A FURTHER QUESTION

The flower blossomed
And the fragrance spread
          and then what?

The waves rose up
And the tide came in
          and then what?

The bird flew
And its cry floated down
          and then what?

(translated from Gujarati by Sujata Bhatt)

Sometimes,
A tree enters
My being
No sooner do I start blossoming
Than the connection is severed at the roots
And one by one
Each leaf yellows,
Falls—
      khar
      khar .

Please,
Never ever talk to me of Spring.

(translated from Gujarati by Panna Naik)

MEMCHOUBI
(ARAMBAM ONGBI IBEMHAL)

THE GODDESS OF LIGHTNING*

If your spirit hears or not
If you agree or not
I am
The answer you've been searching for, for centuries.
Do you perceive me
As a skylark
Floating freely in the moonlight
Or the glistening dew
Gathered in the tender buds of roses
Blooming in the early morning?
No, I am none of these
I am the Goddess of Lightning
The Goddess of Lightning.
Hearing the thunder of my voice
This old earth surely will collapse.
These two rotten arms of yours
That you've preserved so preciously
By painting them with new colours
Stretching them out like some hero
Towards the gate to a new history
I shall burn them
In the thousand-tongued fire of my glance
I shall burn
The burden of your rusted ideas
Of many centuries.
While you stand frozen
At my hideous form
I shall finish
Creating the earth anew.

---

* The Goddess of Lightning (Nongthang Leima) is associated with the myth of the creation of the Earth by the Meitei.

(translated from Manipuri by L. Joychandra Singh)

JYOTSNA MILAN

WIND-TREE

I

I lifted my eyes
And saw
The wind in front of me
And she was showing me a tree
Here see!
This is a tree
This
Is what a tree is like!

II

Giggling
Suddenly
The room
Was drenched in green laughter
Standing on tiptoe
I peeked outside
The wind was tickling the tree
And the tree
Was laughing out loud!

III

I paused
Near the tree
The wind
Had grabbed the branches
And was swinging
In the wind.

IV

The wind
Was teaching the tree to speak
Say 's'

In Their Own Voice

Say '*k*'
Say '*y*'
The tree repeated after her.
The words were the wind's
The tree said them.

V

After running endlessly
The wind rested
Leaning against the tree
And the tree
Stood watching her
Eyes unblinking.

(translated from Hindi by Mrinal Pande and Arlene Zide)

WOMAN – 2

Sometimes
In the moments of lovemaking
The man seems god-like to the woman
    'God . . . God!'
The woman calls out
Her body
Set on fire
    'Look,'
The man says
    'I'm God.'
The woman
Looks
and
Convulsing with the pain of losing God
Turns her face away.

(translated from Hindi by Mrinal Pande and Arlene Zide)

SANGHAMITRA MISHRA

SORROW

Sorrow is the money-lender
Who sits on the doorstep.
You keep on repaying,
But can never pay him off.
The debt keeps mounting
Day by day.
Is there no escape?

You try to jump past the circle
But only break your bones in a fall.
In the race
It is sorrow which sprints ahead of you
And reaches the goalpost first.

Sorrow is the goldfish,
Beautiful to behold in your net
But when you try to catch it
Slips away.

It is sorrow which waits for you,
At the door, like your mother.
Sorrow sits near the Garuda* pillar,
Its fragrance wafts below the throne of God.
Omnipotent sorrow!
We, the humble subjects
Of its kingdom.

And for those it loves, sorrow makes its own
For them, it worries more than death.
It doesn't care if you are father
Son friend wife
In its reign, day and night are equal.
A perpetual deluge, a twelve-month monsoon
An uncontrollable stream.

---

* There is usually a Garuda, the mythological bird-vehicle (vahana) of the god, Vishnu, in front of a temple pillar.

In Their Own Voice

All eyes have lost their luster
Sleepless, without food, burdened like donkeys.
Numberless sighs pent up within their chests
They are the subjects.
For them, the royal words are joyful,
Sorrow the only obedience,
Another name for life,
And history tells a tale of sorrow
Its colours fast, growing deeper every day.

Yashoda, scatters a handful of rice
Before the sacred crow,
So he'll return.*

---
* There is a belief in Orissa that if the crow caws, you can expect a guest.
  Yashoda is Krishna's mother.

(translated from Oriya by J. P. Das and Arlene Zide)

SUCHETA MISHRA

DISTANCE

A poet is a chunk of sky
A painter tossing a handful of stars
There too, sorrow falls into a design
And for that reason the sky is beautiful
And the poet beautiful.
No, don't ask the poet for the cause
Of her grief, her agony and despair
Or ever probe the signs of her silence
Hers is such a heart, where
From veranda to the house
There is a flow of grief and pain.

No, don't stretch out your hand
Your palm is too small for her wounds
And if you say so, like the spring breeze
Her touch will softly caress your brow.
But the day your shadow fell on her heart
The trampled footprints of the world's griefs
Left their mark upon her.
And the day she suddenly found out she was a 'poet'
From that very day her death began.
No, don't stretch out your hand
A poet is a chunk of sky
Say, how can you ever touch her.

(translated from Oriya by Jayanta Mahapatra)

YASHODHARA MISHRA

THE SEA

There is no escape from the sea.
Sometimes,
When you're not watching
It snatches things from your hands.
Sometimes, at your feet
It washes up
The things you'd thrown away.

Or else, those cheap earrings
A little girl once had lost,
Bathing in the sea,
Had grieved over,
And in the end, forgotten—
After an age, the sea
Washes up again.

(translated from Oriya by J. P. Das and Arlene Zide)

DEBARATI MITRA

PALOMA COLLEGE

This year no dust gathered during the summer break
On the tables and chairs of the closed room.
The long locked-up vacation filled
        with the whirring of birds' wings.
The window sills piled up with songs, divine
        mathematics, luxuriant descriptions,
A magician with a hat for catching rabbits.
Whatever he snared turned into faces,
Heads that end at the shoulders,
Nothing below.
But they're so beautiful I'm not afraid.

Listen to the mandolin in the fresh light
        swirling like stirred carrot soup
And in the depths of the young girl's dance.
Foliage from the strumming trees dissolves
        into the water of the pond
Where the dark bulges like a fish's eye.
I don't care to blow alphabet bubbles any longer,
Pages of my books like chrysalises just awakened
Pushing through the cocoons and flowing
        into the wind.

This year in the locked room during the summer break
Not a speck of dust collected.

(translated from Bengali by Paramita Banerjee and Carolyne Wright)

APARNA MOHANTY

What do you see
Looking at me like this?
Checking whether or not I resemble
Poetry's muse?
With which ornaments bedecked,
In what style my hair arranged?
If I'll sparkle
Exactly
Like that doll in your imagination?
Perhaps that thought
Has brought a new glint to your eyes
Or
Undressing the coy maiden
In your mind,
You drag me
To that temple of love, the bridal chamber—
The pen slips
Describing breasts and hips,
Thoughts become
The lolling tongues of desire.

God!
From birth I've been brought up
In the blind well of ignorance,
Small-mindedness,
Happy always
To have offered into your hands
This rare womanhood,
My touchstone body
For weighing,
For your judgment,
Like some fresh-cut piece of meat.

I've stayed pure
I've accepted
That it's my nature
To stay pure,
Even if I have no other

In Their Own Voice

Respectable identity
But that of ovary
Approved by you.

That I can think,
Can feel;
That a special touch of the soul
Can redeem
My frame of flesh and blood;
Can claim *paramarth,* the supreme meaning
Can achieve the *moksha* of salvation,
That this body
Is not
A silk-clad statue or a fly
Caught in a spider's web,
That this body can lift its head
And tower
Like a sky-touching temple
Of knowledge and consciousness,
Often
Waking to this possibility
In raised voice saying this aloud
I've stopped,
From some odd fear
Kept silent,
Even though much earlier
Should have spoken out.

I would have said, addressing you alone—
Take off your mask,
Off with it!
What sort of friend are you?
What sort of soul-mate?
Kind of companion?
What kind of partner
On life's journey?
Shame on you!
From history's beginnings
I have had to take as men

In Their Own Voice

Carnivorous dogs and tigers
Shackled in the chains
Of rank and status,
Shame! On me!
Unable
To say this openly,
Imprisoned in some enchantment,
Entangled in illusion.

So with bent head
I listen
Always
To my own suppressed pitiful cries
Shame on me!
A hundred times more so than on you.
Feeling that this is all that I deserve,
Believing myself to be
The lowliest of the low,
Giving myself over
To the accursed half of the world.
Shame, and shame again!
A hundred times more
On me!

(translated from Oriya by J. P. Das and Arlene Zide)

BRAHMOTRI MOHANTY

FAITH

If you loved somebody before our marriage
And if that memory still burns
Or if, despite my closeness
Some new infatuation
Has been creating rainbows in your heart
I am not sad about it, I just have one request—
Please keep that secret
Secret and don't let me know.
Let me keep my faith in you unbroken
—(Unnecessary inquisitiveness means death).

Of this golden world of sapphires, pearls and diamonds
I am queen.
Why should I set my calm and certain mind afire
With sick psychology, distorted judgements, useless doubts?
You love me deeply—
Has anyone ever loved with such intensity?

When you return home in the dead of night
Having committed a terrible sin
Please tell me you were listening
To the Ramayana.

(translated from Oriya by Sulekha Samantaray and Arlene Zide)

GIRIBALA MOHANTY

GOOD NEWS BAD NEWS

I'm telling it the way it happened.
This is the way the world is now.

Disease sorrow hunger in every house.
At the end of the month of *magha*
If it rains it's good for the king
Good for the land.
But this *magha* the heavy downpour
Wreaked havoc
The winter crop damaged
Disease in every house.

And here before month's end
Your pay packet finished.
The rations too.
Shortages everywhere.
It'll be a shame
If spring comes now.
What will it think
Seeing such disease, such poverty, such sorrow?
Straining to feed a hungry belly
Who has the time
To welcome it with the *gundakeri* raga?
Where is the place
To write a welcome message
Or lay out a spread?
At the foot of a tree, on the footpath,
At the bottom of a drain, on the office veranda?
These are not fit places
For a visit from the prince of seasons.

(translated from Oriya by J. P. Das and Arlene Zide)

NIRMALA MOHANTY

THE PEDLAR

The pedlar of happiness
Basket on his head,
Hawks his wares, his voice
Overflowing into the streets
Of Vrindavan, Mathura and Dwaraka.
The leafless *kadamba* tree has budded
And the water ripples
In the Yamuna of the mind.

Who are you, pedlar?
Where is your home?
What is your name?
What pleasures have you brought to sell,
That, lusting after, I rush in and out of this house,
Like a madwoman.

Tell me the truth, pedlar
You wouldn't cheat me
In the name of happiness?
My life's strings are bound
To the four walls
Sorrow its relentless fate.
I'm but a basket of that sorrow,
A verse of despair.

I'm a respectable woman, pedlar
I've crossed the threshold
And now stand
Upon the streets
Leaving behind family and caste,
My rank and honour.
At the magic of your call
Have run out
Into the open.

My straying feet won't return home, pedlar.
Honour once damaged cannot be repaired.

In Their Own Voice

When a dream palace is shattered
The way a glass doll breaks, it can't be fixed.

What spell then have you cast
That I go running blindly, after you?
What raga are you singing
That shakes the very soul
And jolts the universe?

Hold on, pedlar,
I'll buy all the happiness in your basket,
At the price of my mind,
Paying for it with my grief.
I might lose everything in this deal,
But then who cares?
Let our bargain,
This profit and loss
Live for ever.

(translated from Oriya by J. P. Das and Arlene Zide)

SASMITA MOHANTY

MISTRESS

I

Rippling
Jumping, running
Over thorny ground
A tomboy brook
Its destination
Far away
Far, very far . . .

II

On the carpet of the grassy lawn
Slowly
Gathering
Drops of dew
Alluring as a diamond
Dazzling, but
Adds oil
To the fire of thirst.

(translated from Oriya by J. P. Das and Arlene Zide)

WIFE

I

In the posture of surrender
A peaceful, still, full river
Laughingly bears
The brunt of paddle and oar,
Is not troubled by
The ocean's fearsome roar.

In Their Own Voice

II

In the courtyard
A small well
Full with sweet cold water
Whenever you need it,
There to quench your thirst.

(translated from Oriya by J. P. Das and Arlene Zide)

KANCHANKUNTALA MUKHERJEE

ALONG THE RAILROAD TRACK

In our childhood days,
On the way to our country place
We could see the paddy fields stretching for miles
Patterned with red spinach.
A vast expanse of green,
Lush with crops, and more crops.
The eternal wag-tailed swallow
Perched on the telegraph wires
The farmer in the drizzling rain
Palm-leaf hat upon his head
And many more wonders
Waiting
Along the railway track.
Today, many years later

Even more sinister wonders
Wait along the track,
These days a new addition—
A harvest of violent clashes
Nights,
Along the slippery ridges of the paddy fields
Where the field-snake lies relaxed among the dewdrops
Hearing the familiar footsteps of the farmer,
Slips away into the field.
There,
Near the railway station of Belanagar or of Pandua
Besides the iron rails
The headless corpse of a young boy lies.
And, in future years, grimmer wonders
Await us.

In Their Own Voice

Rumour has it—
A strange new red spinach pattern will be woven
With the blood of a young farmboy.

Note: This poem refers to the peasant uprisings in the 60's and 70's; also to sporadic movements later, when farmers refused to give up their harvest to the zamindari landowners.

(translated from Bengali by Paramita Banerjee and Arlene Zide)

VIJAYA MUKHOPADHYAY

COMPANION

The one with whom we always live
Is not called love, but worry
Love, like a visitor,
Drops in sometimes, with the slightest of smiles,
Leaves mementos behind all over the house,
Then in a flash disappears.

After that, all the time,
Some of us and worry,
One of us and worry,
Live in the house together
From night to day, day to night.

(translated from Bengali by Sunil B. Ray and Carolyne Wright with the author)

ADVERTISEMENT

Abortion is possible up to five times—
That's what the ad says.

Then why cry
After this sixth-week abortion, wife,
With your nipples turned tender-dark
As new leaves?
A red palm scouring your womb,
Eclipsing the hunger of mother-love
Fiend of a woman, nature won't stand for it!
Your foetus-daughter will return, again, again,
Forcing you, eager, anxious,
Back each time to that clinic's stench.

Note: The writer uses the form *tui* (similar to the French *tu*) to refer to the woman in the poem. It is a form of address that at once suggests intimacy, insult, rage.

(translated from Bengali by Chitra Banerjee Divakaruni with editing by the author and Arlene Zide)

MUKTHAYAKKA

LITTLE POEMS

I

Raindrops
dropping one by one
from a tree,
memories of the night
I spent with you.

II

Only when you left me
in cold December,
did I remember
the blanket
put away,
tied up in a bundle.

III

When your first kisses
wrote in silence
my name all over
my body,
in that stillness
silence began to sing.

IV

I'm the candle
I've lit with the fire
in your eyes
and in memory
I burn, I melt.

In Their Own Voice

V

As you look
at the excitement
in my eyes,
does the cold beer
in your hand
grow warm?

(translated from Kannada by A. K. Ramanujan)

VRINDA NABAR

OXFORD ODE

Perpetual oddity, I
shift from foot to foot
when, twice a month,
I'm broiled and grilled by
Moral Tutor Miss D.
Elsewhere,
crab-apple dons, sex
confined to their eyes
smile on me with fatherly interest
and offer sherry
mild as their ancient wives.

Strangers stop me on the Broad
to ask if Maharishi
wrote the *Kamasutra*.
Raw, blonde boys
flaunt me in Junior Common Rooms.

They're never sure
how the sari-clad
take to being kissed.
Some make the attempt.
others (most of them)
shake hands and leave
to booze it off.

Guy Fawkes night.
I bump a drunk
who mutters 'Filthy Wog'.

I find him at the next meeting
of the Joint Action Committee
Against Racial Intolerance.

I learn:
It's trendy to be bored.
I say:

In Their Own Voice

'How boring!'
at unlikely moments.
Going Down
is also Going Home:
St. Anne's, for ever

an optical illusion.

LALITHA NAIK

SMALL CHANGE

Paisa by paisa, I was growing,
not into a ten or a hundred rupee note,
perhaps, but into a single one.
But then, my friend, you tied the marriage-knot
and started turning me into small change.

My brains, skills and talent,
you have decided, are to make secure
a feeling of well-being in your belly and head.
Incensed, I look for words
stronger than 'Down with . . .'
to condemn your age-old belief
that my limbs are for the pleasure of your senses.

I am amazed that you value more
your whiskers than my breasts
that burst with life-nourishing milk.
I am waiting, waiting, wanting
to whisper into your ears
that, if your fatherhood is just a part
of your life, so too is my motherhood.

(translated from Kannada by Ramachandra Sharma)

PANNA NAIK

SEED

With open eyes and closed lips
questions haunt me
misty at midnight;
oh mother,
now in the morning
with open eyes and open lips
I ask you
the way a close friend would.

Mother,
tell me
did you take off
your mind's garments
at the time of your copulation?
Was the only window
open or shut?
Was it a night
of full moon?
Was it a darkling night
with twinkling stars?
Did your eyes
relax and communicate?
Did your lips
taste each others' embracing smiles?
Did your cheeks
radiate red?
Were your bodies touched by
the fragrance of the fully blossomed night queen?
Was your orgasm
the climax
of your union
or
did you fake it
to end it
all?

In Their Own Voice

Even after you say 'yes'
to all but the last question
why do I feel
as if
you two had sown
the seed of pain
in your moment of orgasm?

(translated from Gujarati by the author)

TALK

All our lives
we
talked and talked and talked
about the living room.
I wish
at least once
at least one day, one night,
we had
talked
about the bedroom . . .

(translated from Gujarati by the author)

PRATIBHA NANDAKUMAR

POEM

When I was groping for a new poem
for the poetry festival,
poems danced all over the house:
in nooks and corners, in the bed,
in boxes, in walls and curtains,
in windows and doors
poems beckoned with their hands.
They simmered on the stove
in the *rasam* pot, got flattened
under the rolling pins
on the chapati stone,
and diced on the knife-stand
they boiled in the cooker
with salt and spices,
sautéed, smelling fragrant.

In the hall they were lying about
begging to be picked up.
If I swept them, they asked
to be mopped; if I mopped them,
they wanted to be dressed,
stubborn pests, thorns
in my flesh.
Curtains where little hands
had wiped themselves,
torn books, sandals dropped,
chairs and tables pulled here and there,
clothes strewn on the floor
took on the shapes of poems
and dazzled my eyes.

When I cleared the mess
and sat down to rest,
one of them pestered me
asking me now to wash it,
now to give it a drink,

In Their Own Voice

now to come play with it.

When at last I sat down to write
not one letter got written
and my brain was in a fog.
Late at night, when a sleepy hand
groped and hugged me
'To hell with the poem,' I said
and fell asleep.
But it tickled me in a dream,
made me laugh and charmed me.

When I read that
in the poetry festival,
it ran out, refused to come back,
went inside the listeners and sat there.
I let it sit there
and came home alone.

(translated from Kannada by A. K. Ramanujan)

TEJASWINI NIRANJANA

PICTURES

*poems for unredeemed kinship
for my grandmother*

I

This
is the only picture we have
She believed such things
diminished
our days

But this was
her son's wedding

The three of them
in a studio
with black curtains
for a backdrop

The last
rains rotted the young
people's faces

Only my grandmother
remains
in the centre
on a folding chair—
bone already gleaming
beneath the parched skin,
her head
under the sari's edge
shaped like mine.

II

Friday nights she would roast
small white onions,
plucking them from the coals
with her fingers—
they lay
like crumpled jasmine
in the cups of our palms
Hearts like pebbles scrubbed by the sea

This is what she did as a girl
on monsoon nights
while fishing boats
reared at anchor, palm trees
arched in the wind

Still her coal stove burns
She continues to fast for Shiva
on the eleventh day of the waxing moon

Thirty years away from the sea
in the midst of red buses and girls on bicycles
she who never learned to tell a clock's time
imagines returning oxen
and the nets of reapers

She guards rice cakes from
the wheeling crows
without throwing a pebble
and grows bushes of jasmine for the lord

III

Me she never carried—
the mesh of wrinkles on her hip
had unremembered the weight of children

never touched—
to clean
or heal
my hopscotch wounds
Every month under the mango tree,
outside, a bearded barber
shaved her head
as she heard with troubled eyes
the wild parrots peck the growing fruit
and the children
predatory among the leaves

Once a year
at Deepavali
I chalked flowers and lamps
on her water heater,
listening for fireworks
to burn the night away

Once a year
while I read from the almanac
in front of her gods
in a language neither hers nor mine
I felt the treebark fingers
trembling on my head,
as she stroked coconut oil with a neem twig
through the length of my hair

IV

Ten years old, she was married
to one who lived by the sea

The water, lapping at her childhood,
murmured all day
under the skin

Today it hurtles
in my blood,
I who saw the crabs
scutter in the fine sand
only two weeks each summer

Home from school
I'd sometimes get
her beaten rice
doused in water
sprinkled with salt

I'd see the ridges
where salt glistened dully
in the sun,
where
after her husband died
she'd beg the saltmakers
for the rough brown grains

My arteries
lined with salt
contract
with thirst to remember
ancestors to appease

In Their Own Voice

V

All the gold pawned,
she joined the other widows
to wash clothes
for brahmin households
and winnow the grain
in gaunt doorways,
swinging the separator
with unjewelled arms

Each month, my mother and I
would crouch with her,
wordless, picking brown stones
from rice to be stored

Her mind runs
through the thirsty blades
where toadstools
nudge the ashen dirt

Demon birds
swoop
on the strips of dried mango
she watches over
all summer long

Sitting on the doorstep,
her wrinkled dugs
bared to the sun, she listens
to the clack of bracelets
as I swirl rice grains
in a pan of water,
charming the stones
to the surface.

KONDEPUDI NIRMALA

LABOUR ROOM

The moment you enter
the labour room
you see inferno in 3-D:
either hell on earth
or the earth in hell.

A river of pain on each table.
Hands stifling screams.
Cries, calls.
Howls. Yowls.
Throes. Spasms.
All normal, quite normal.

Walking, talking, laughing
and such, and all biological features
get a new form here.
What counts is a cry, or at least a moan.

Legs spread wide helplessly,
looking forward to the climactic crest
of cataclysm,
like a coin crushed flat and wide
on the rails by the wheels of a train.
Sawdust wound as a ball
given to the blade of the saw.

No room to think.
No deadline between life and death.
Maybe the fish on the hook writhes like this.
Maybe a dumb animal trussed in a sack cries like this.

Well, this is not the end.
Much depends on pain, more pain.
This is yesterday's case:
the pulse is weak.
That is the latest case:
the foetus is transverse.

In Their Own Voice

Still nothing happens to you.
Wait, wait for the clock
to turn on its hours.

Look, there she comes, full term,
by bus, car, rickshaw, and on foot.
A saline bottle upside down
to give away life drop by drop.

(translated from Telugu by the author and edited by A. K. Ramanujan)

JAMEELA NISHAT

I

I turned Eve
To pervade
Your being,
You became my Adam.

Eyes tore
Through clothes
Silence rustled
Between my thighs
A serpent
Crept into my heaven.
The tree melted
Drop by drop,
A spring broke out
In my body's vale.

II

On a green hill
I stand
Holding a yellow water pot.
In the dim distance
A caravan moves.
The plodders are thirsty
My pail of water
Has turned into a green lake
The travellers ache for water
The lake is poisoned.
The caravan has gone to sleep.
Overhead, bats hover.

In Their Own Voice

III

The din of voices
Dies slowly in the alley of Death.
Love, that until yesterday
Raged in my limbs
Is now stilled in my breast.
You recede from me
I from you
Each distancing the other,
The storm faints in death's tunnel,
The winds of estrangement
Sting,
You are 'you' again
And I,
I too
Begin to wear my ego on my sleeve.

IV

Down the winding alley of time
Where are you going?
What do you seek?
Why do you peer
Into the ravaged maternal womb?
What do you hope to see?

The red spread across this page
Is not the red of roses,
Not the blood of Jesus either
To wash away your sins.
This deep-hued red
Is life itself.

See—the road lies shattered.
Don't venture in the alley
Where souls are clothed
In the weeds of Death
And volcanoes sleep in the bones.

In Their Own Voice

Do not call out or wake anyone,
If you wish to listen,
Listen to the hooting owls
On the bare-limbed tree,
Listen
To their story
But tell no one
For they're all asleep.

(translated from Urdu by Syed Sirajuddin)

MRINAL PANDE

TWO WOMEN KNITTING

Rama said
Rama said to Uma
Oh my,
How time passes.
Ah me, says Uma
and then both fall silent.

The two women cast on stitches
Skip stitches, slip the skipped stitches over,
Knit over purl,
Purl over knit.
After many intricate loops and cables
Their dark secrets still lie locked within
They have thrown the keys to their jewel casques in the lake.
Put the keys in, and their locks will bleed real blood.

Two women are knitting
Clicking steel against steel
Passers-by look up amazed at the sparks that fly.
Loneliness comes at every other row in their patterns
Though they have worn each others' saris
And bathed each others' slippery infants
Even though at this very moment their husbands
Lie asleep in the rooms upstairs
Shaking them in their dreams.

(*translated from Hindi by the author and Arlene Zide*)

In Their Own Voice

HER HOME

Every day
Before the crow of the cock and the thud of the newspaper
In that no-man's land between the law and the blood
The woman gives birth to her separate world.

The clay pots are her sons,
Clever and cheeky
The tongs clang their palms together on command
The matchstick immediately sputters into flame
While the brass pot bubbles over with curiosity
And the ladle slowly mashes the secret-filled greens.

That homebody, the hanging pot loves curling up
The rotund rolling pin rolls over laughing
Coiled up and irritable, *chhichchirchhikk!*
The narrow whisk prances around.

Here with a single calculated blow
The woman can behead four okra pods
Can slit open the heart of a bitter gourd
Then throwing a magic pinch of red chilli into cast-iron depths
She can create a smoking, spluttering hell.

Spotless, the radish stands like a gigantic exclamation point
Watches the woman sitting
With her back to the hard wall
And wonders, really,
How real is she?

(translated from Hindi by the author and Arlene Zide)

UMA PARAMESWARAN

I WISH I KNEW WHAT TO TELL YOU, MY DAUGHTERS

Hoping to steal a catnap
While my host's child drew her crayons
Across pages of my story,
    where lovers at the edge of estrangement
    and I at an impasse where to take them next,
I said, Tell me a story, Duggi.

And I heard through catnapping ears,
'Baddu got mad at me . . .
We played . . . and Baddu was mad
at me . . . I wanted CareBear and
. . . Baddu got mad at me . . . he came back
from school and Baddu got mad at me . . .'

Seeking to stop this litany against her brother
Away at their grandma's on long vacation,
I said, 'Tell me a happy story, Duggi, a happy one.'

And she sing-sang said, 'Baddu pushed me . . . I told him
I wanted to stay at grandma's with him . . .
And Baddu pushed me . . . Baddu . . .'
No, no, Duggi, tell me how
(and I guessed at random)
Baddu found your Big Bird that'd got thrown away
Or shared with you his caramel sundae . . .

Opening my eyes at the long pause
That had snaked over the room, I saw Duggi,
Her eyes bright with tears, and she cried,
'I want Baddu HERE NOW, I WANT BADDU.'

Possible Endings:

a.   Duggi, my baby, should I warn you
    this is the oldest trap of all? or do I feel so
    Only because that ending would not sell my story
    Where it counts?

b. Duggi, my baby, I lured you into the oldest trap of all—
When Eve turned away and said,
Your God is not for me, I shall go my way . . .
Adam stroked her hair and murmured,
Remember all the good times we've had,
The times we wandered naming all creatures
Of water and land and sky, each named by us;
The times I held your hand when you were in pain;
The good times,
the warm times,
times of togetherness,
the good times we've had together
the good times we've had
the good times we
the good times
the good . . .
And Eve remembered and stayed
and followed
and obeyed
and slaved
and died
and was born again and again and again
my daughters, And told you in turn
To remember the good times.
Remember, dismember, mismember.

c. I wish I knew what to tell you, Duggi, my baby,
If fate should have you say that of another
Than your brother, should I ask you to remember
dismember mismember encumber your self?
Or should I lure you into another fork in the road

172

In Their Own Voice

>And risk you to fall again and again and again
>Into lonely remembrance
>Or promiscuous abandon
>Or lonely aloneness
  In the hope you will go your way
  From strength to strength?

Note: The first part of this poem is for Rakhi, the annual Hindu festival where brothers and sisters pledge mutual love and support, affirming sibling bonds that, the poem says, can never be broken. The second part turns upon the persona—her reaction on recognizing that she has played a role in the child's reaction, and generally on the role of counsellors.

GEETA PARIKH

THERE IS JOY

There is joy, there is my child
and tonight,
a party to celebrate the birth.
I'm having the large drawing room cleaned out,
the cobwebs swept away.

'Look, that pigeon
has laid some eggs!'
My servant shouts.

'Remove the nest.
It'll stink up the whole place.'

'Please take out the trash.
Everything is in it now, the nest
the eggs—I've got it all ... '

I take all this 'dirt'
and dump it outside.

Before I can even come back
in, the two eggs
are snatched away by crows.

I start scrubbing out
the spot where the nest
had lain. But the mother pigeon
doesn't *budge*
and her eyes, full of pain
don't move.

Finally, I have her
pushed out with a stick
until she's forced to fly away.

In Their Own Voice

And then, I ask for everything
to be cleaned again—
I, who am full of joy
because of my child's birth.

(translated from Gujarati by Sujata Bhatt)

RAJANI PARULEKAR

THE SNAKE COUPLE

A sound . . .
Stiff in the scorching afternoon
. . . Slightly wet
. . . Moist, gradually gathering in the evening
. . . Spread, like *Jaswandi* petals
Deep red,
the center stamen somewhat bent,
entreating.

How often has that sound dragged you
You closed your doors
Even so, like an arrow shooting straight through your thigh
its echoes pierced the walls and surrounded them.

At each meeting you walked very fast
with the same speed, you spoke and spoke
from the depths of your inner mind . . . as if talking to yourself.

And once . . .
near the uninhabited, tumbledown house
in the brimming silence
The wind hidden away in the hollow of the sky
Sound became hot, rushing passion.
If only a leaf had fallen in the water
countless ripples would have arisen,
and the snake-couple, playfully roving on the green grass
could have stood upon their tails,   erect.

(translated from Marathi by Asha Mundlay and Arlene Zide)

A TORRENT OF PEOPLE AND WORDS

A torrent of people, a torrent of words,
at the office, in the vegetable market,
in the queue for the bus,
around the sugarcane press,

words of welcome, words of urging:
from behind the words peer
subtle hatred, dormant selfishness,
sympathy
(for the wrong reason),
sometimes wounded egotism,
sometimes pure curiosity:
because of them
people's wretched, rotten lives
brighten up for a moment!

A torrent of people, a torrent of words...
pressing words, inviting words,
like the partly-nibbled peas
inside a plump pod:
the green of the pod,
the green of the peas,
the green of the nibbling parasite.

Thirsty, one feels thirsty then,
thirsty for big, detached, knowledgeable words:
at the sugarcane press
glasses fill up with juice, empty out,
there's laughter, joking... the horns of cars...
the heap of crushed sugarcane...
the glasses empty out... one feels thirsty.

The glasses fill up again... one feels thirsty.
The froth of the juice
spreads everywhere like a swirl of mist.
The surge of people, the honking of cars
seem like things in a picture.
All that's left
is the tinkling of the small brass bells
tied to the wheels of the press,
and my eyes brim, remembering you.

(translated from Marathi by Vinay Dharwadker)

ANURADHA PATIL

SQUARE-KNOT

The chinking bangles bought after her pestering at the village
                                                   fair, forgotten.
The girls with unkempt tresses, romping round the tree-bench,
                                                        forgotten.
The bride starts to leave.
Accompanied by the halter tied upon her neck.

Oh woman!   Pour a little water over her
Turmeric-smeared feet.
This is the forsaken time
When no one belongs to you.

    You can't die, really
    Following in the footsteps of one already dead.

But just watch—
How, from now on
From within their innermost core,
Her days will change.

(translated from Marathi by Asha Mundlay and Arlene Zide)

HEMA PATTANASHETTI

A VOICE

Monkeys leap on the tree
and play havoc.
All day church bells
ring in the distance.
The marketplace hunts
for better rates.
Through the drums and the noise
of lies and tricks,
through the ambush,
I've to become a mere voice,
a call
that gets a hearing,
reaches everyone
in a new time.

(translated from Kannada by A. K. Ramanujan)

ANURADHA POTDAR

MOTHERHOOD

Just once
I wanted to leave the garments of my motherhood on the riverbank
Enter the bottomless waters of life
Just once
Like a small bird, spreading its wings toward the sky
I wanted to bathe in that clear blue
Just once.

Not the way, entering a stream, you leave your clothes along the bank
But the way you'd drag,
Scrape off that old hunchback riding on your neck.
Just for one moment put aside this motherhood
That some time back had climbed upon my shoulders.

In a cruel burst of passion, I threw away those clothes
Which scorched my every limb.
Plunging into the clear open stream
I let out one unburdened breath of freedom.
From every particle of my being, a delicate echo replied
Just for a moment.
I realized, in less than a moment
What I'd left behind on the bank were not the garments of my
                                                    motherhood
But naive self-deception.
That motherhood had tightly bound me, like the skin along
                                                    every limb

At once
Nurturing me, supporting me
And
Pushing me into neverending, bottomless pain.
—It was never going to leave me
I was never going to say no to it!

(translated from Marathi by Asha Mundlay and Arlene Zide)

AMRITA PRITAM

VIRGIN

When I stepped into your bridal chamber
I was not one—but two
One completely wedded, one completely chaste ....
For the sake of your pleasure—
I had to kill that virgin
So I killed her—
These murders, legitimate by law
Only the humiliation of them illegitimate
I drank the poison of that humiliation.
Then the morning came—
And saw my hands all wet with blood.
I washed my hands—
Just the way I washed your musty man-smell from my body
But when I came before the mirror
There she was before me
The very one I'd murdered in the night
Oh! God!
Had the darkness of the bridal chamber been so dense?
Which one had I come to kill, which one had I killed ....

(translated from Punjabi by Arlene Zide with the author.

CREATIVE PROCESS

The poem looks at the paper
And turns her face away
As if the paper were a strange man, not her own.

But, when a virgin keeps the fast of *karva chauth**
And on that dreamlike night
Senses a male touch in a dream
Suddenly, her body shivers.

---

* a fast kept by married women for the well-being of their husbands, broken a the first sighting of the moon in the evening.

But, sometimes, tasting that fire
Startled, she awakes.
She touches her lush body
and undoes her blouse,
Splashes a handful of moonlight over her body.
Her hand sobs as she dries her body.

The darkness of her body spreads out like a mat.
Lying face down on the mat, she picks at straws
Every limb of her body catches fire.
She feels as though her body's darkness longs
To be crushed in powerful arms.

Suddenly, paper appears before her
And touches her trembling hands
One part of her body burns,
Another melts
She senses a strange odour
And her hand reads the throbbing lines of her body.
Her hands grow drowsy
Her body becomes a total stranger.
She breaks into a cold sweat

A long line breaks—
Her breath is drenched in the smell of life and death.
All these thin, black lines
Like pieces of a drawn-out scream.

Silent, puzzled
Drained
She stands and looks
As if some injustice had been committed
Some small part of her had died
As if a virgin had conceived,
And then miscarried.

(translated from Punjabi by the author and Arlene Zide)

SAVITRI RAJEEVAN

THE DAY

My day climbed the steps
opening the closed gate and the door
opening the locked eye and mind
My day.

Milk and water boiled together
to make tea,
Idlis steamed
news hot off the press
having swallowed this much
what should I do now?

With palm leaf and stylus
my child
climbed down the hill
my son, whose hands and feet grow thin
struggling with his lessons.

Maria,
my maid-servant
who has nothing
to sow or reap
went to church
with prayer and hope.
With my two eyes
stretching towards both past and future
I sit alone.

Day.

Loneliness
sharp-edged as the day:
the wind which has come down from the clouds
this mid-day light
leaning on the compound wall
what do they tell me?

In Their Own Voice

Baldy,
crossing the green maidan,
has a glistening head
where the high-noon light
makes its nest.

Beyond the gate
a palmist
his head full of forecasts
has a long tongue and a bird in a cage.
This ancient dog
sleeping with its head on the doorstep
has a shadow with a curved tail.

Without a lesson to learn
or a god to visit
or, for that matter
a shining head or a tail,
I really sit alone.

Opening the closed gate and the door
opening the locked eye and mind
my day
why does it climb the steps?

(translated from Malayalam by Ayyappa Paniker and Arlene Zide)

A PAIR OF GLASSES

It's with glasses
in front of my eyes and on my nose
that I see the world.

I need glasses
to see my neighbour and the washerman
and the postman
to see that Radha and Krishna walking along the road
or to see Radha as Radha
and Krishna as Krishna.

In Their Own Voice

Glasses are the door
through which I talk to a stranger, a guest and a friend.
Through the glass I speak
to children, flowers,
and to God.

Glasses for my daydreams,
and for my cradle-songs.

For my unspoken word
and unsung song
Glasses.
Glasses for me.

In my childhood
I had no glasses.
All great men wear glasses.
All wearers of glasses are great.
My childhood—without glasses.
The textbook Gandhi-ji
The cane-wielding math teacher,
and the postman, Appunni.

Or, for that matter
behind every pair of glasses that are taken off—
A great man.
In my childhood
I had no glasses

Glasses—
Like a halo
for gods and prophets
Like the scholar's baldness
or the potbelly of the prosperous.

Today,
I too have a pair of glasses.

(translated from Malayalam by Ayyappa Paniker and Arlene Zide)

RAJLUKSHMEE DEBEE

COPHETUA

Your voice cracked the shell of the sky.
Your guards bent knees unused
to alley rubble, their arms stiff
under silks and pearls
for you to court my beggar heart.

This love is an entering, an end.
In loving we fall like parched flowers,
or burn blue ice, like stars. I give you
the lines of my hollow palms.

The palace gathers itself around me,
steady, many-chambered as a heart.
I climb white stairs to a roof of fog.
It is dark, this lost world of sphinxes

into which I empty my past, hunger
like an explosion in my skull,
cold like the broken bones' singing.
In my dark hut, that first flash
of your naked rainbow body.

Emperor, your velvets rope my flesh.
Somewhere a bed of rags, empty,
mourns for you and me.

Note: The reader might wish to look at Tennyson's poem, 'Cophetua and the Beggar Maid', which tells the story of the king who, charmed by the beggar maid's beauty, made her his queen.

(translated from Bengali by Chitra Banerjee Divakaruni)

NITA PRAMOD RAMAIYA

THE YEAR OF 1979

This is the year
Of my mother's glance up through the water
At all of us
Submitting the joys and sorrows of 68 years to the Machhu River.
This is the year
of my brother's last scream
Hoarding his 23 years in the flood waters
overflowing in his sparkling eyes and shining shoes.
This is the year
That made
Study Literature Politics Ideologies
Understanding Intelligence Wisdom stammer.
How can I explain to my son
Lighting the courtyard of my parents' house
That I am being pounded, pounded
At every step I take within this house?
This is the year
Of the invisible scene hanging
Between
The mood of my ten-year-old son
And
My devastation.
This is the year
Of the thirst of the shameless
Deranged river.

Note: In 1979, the Morvi dam collapsed and the Machhu river flooded inhabited areas.

(translated from Gujarati by the author)

In Their Own Voice

A YOUNG WOMAN'S RESOLUTION TO PROTECT HERSELF

Whatever is said
        with a thorny tongue
is true
when will people understand that . . .

I'm not one of the extras
in a blue movie
or that heroine
gradually exposed naked in the mirror . . .

For that lover
        in a dark tunnel
after smooth round hillocks of flesh—
and I like a bird
        sliced open . . .
That's not how I want to waste my life.

My youth
is not like some disease
caused by a virus . . .

Not a fish
        lying rotten
by the edge of the sea
for some stray dog to sniff at . . .

The relationship
        that hovers
between beer
        and salted peanuts;

whisky
        and soda
over with a burp.

A restaurant is not home
and where a place isn't home
there love is a delusion
there love cannot dwell.

In Their Own Voice

Household love,
a home overflowing with love
is what I want.

Not just the play, the drama,
but the living green love
of a play-filled home
is what I want.

In the icy seas
of the North pole
      of the South pole,
he who prays to the throb
      of his warmth-giving blood—
that's the one I choose.

(translated from Gujarati by Sujata Bhatt)

ANURADHA RAMANAN

THE VERDICT

the bald-headed
judge
who dismissed
the case
since there weren't
enough witnesses
said this
to a woman
who had gone astray
and stood on the stand
meant for the accused:

'Madam,
don't make
another mistake
like this again!
The police
won't fail to catch you!
You cannot
cheat
the scales
of justice . . .

let that be.
If you are
free
this evening,
why don't you come
to my place?
There's not a soul
in the house
save for me.'

(translated from Tamil by Martha Ann Selby and K. Paramasivam)

C. VIMALA RAO

A SCENE

A morning mist-swirled as Sidonian glass
by a panting breath
the sun was an immortal wound between light-torn rays;

In a hole hidden under the bridge
in public secrecy a husband and wife
rise from dream-sheeted sleep, stir with life;

The man adjusts his dhoti
generously imprinted with pictured gods fully blown
sets out to measure the day by cutting stone;

The woman curved in the daring of a sculpted *apsara*
mirrors her uncontrollable face, shapes her hair like a sexy thing
then adjusts her soul to a gesture of begging;

Above her the universe gallops
in harsh pursuit of a reluctant climax
another day arranges itself as part of the destiny of this man
                                                                    and woman;

And my foreigner friend asks
do they live in houses with addresses?
do tigers roam the streets at night?

PRATIMA RAY

HARVEST MOON

All of these are burning—
The rice stalk and the festival sari
Of red-bordered silk;
Lotus blossoms, cowrie shells, hair,
The sacrificial basket;
The veins' and arteries' gold ornaments;

An ebullient moon over melting skin.
The rice stalks' bones crack open
As the voracious tongue of fire
Caresses the entire body.
On this great funeral pyre.

A naked woman, her legs spread open
In the wind, licks at the heat
With blossoms of bone in her lap.

Note: All of the literal items named here are part of the offerings made to the goddess Lakshmi during the time of Lakshmi Puja, held every year at the time of Kojagori, the first full moon of autumn. Lakshmi, the goddess of fortune and beauty, is associated with prosperity, goodness and happiness.

(translated from Bengali by Paramita Banerjee and Carolyne Wright)

REVATHI DEVI

THIS NIGHT

If this night passes
Which does not surrender
Even to sleeping pills
If this night passes

The night that spreads
Under my back
Like a bed of arrows
For not compromising with man

The night that flows in my veins
Like blood from palm-leaf thorns
For not compromising with God
If this night passes

Spreading a blanket of light
On the face of honesty
Another day
Another day another night another day

Some time another night another day
If honesty stood naked, smooth
Not finding light
If that night stood without passing

It would pass, it would move away, honestly

(translated from Telugu by Velcheru Narayana Rao and A. K. Ramanujan)

In Their Own Voice

SILALOLITA (STONE TOSSED)

This rock with its red radiance
This blue-white rock
This solid rock
Is a rock all right
But if a raindrop falls
If the sunlight touches it
If a small breeze blows
If the scent of perfume reaches it
It would melt, like affection,
Like compassion, like a human being.

Unknown affectionate sculptor
Invaluable beauty's creator
Accomplished sage marked with the stamp of silence
Being seen, heard, felt
This senseless rock transformed
Itself into a conscious rock
This stone into a woman,
Intoxicated, drunk on love,
Drenched in mist, shining
In moonlight
Delicately tossed by a firm mind
This rock.

(translated from Telugu by V. V. B. Rama Rao)

In Their Own Voice

THE VOICE

I talked all this time
And you listened
To whatever I said
Because I didn't have anything to say

And now
I have something to say
Something passionate
Something I love
Something pure
And when I speak
No one listens

For that reason
Or maybe for some other reason
My voice has gone silent

Maybe because of the intoxication of
Losing oneself
Or the sweetness of pleasure
Or maybe because you won't listen
Anyway
The voice has become silent

But
In this silent voice
There are sighs of love
Of a heart sleeping
At one with itself.

(*translated from Telugu by Velcheru Narayana Rao and A. K. Ramanujan*)

ANURADHA MARWAH ROY

I won't disgrace
my education, your sensible world view
won't wonder whether we love.

Due to
complex processes
psycho-social,
bio-physical
and so on . . . .

But don't say 'make love',
fuck, screw, copulate
whatever else you like.

Intractable vocabulary—yours and mine,
mine nit-picking
yours interchangeable.

Then how come
I absorb meanings from dictionaries,
sponge in connotations
yet remain dry?

Dry, loose, floating lost in my stratosphere
you driving purposefully in your car.

A whole gamut of
bio-social-psycho-physiology
wordlessness
tensed
between our parallel lives.

PADMA SACHDEV

LONG HAIR

They say
A woman with long hair has no happiness in her destiny.
Her mother-in-law's hands
Grow tired as they try to comb her hair.
The hair splits at the ends
So that the tears woven in her hair like pearldrops
Won't roll away.
And as that happens, as they come and go, passers-by
Begin to lose their way.
The woman whose husband
Is not home by dusk
Begins to call the woman with the long hair names.
As she paces up and down in her long corridors
Clutching those long, milk-fed tresses in her fists.

Among women with long hair
Evening is a popular name.
At eveningtime, no married woman
Lets her husband venture out.
Does not even put a longhaired thread to needle.
At eveningtime, even flowing rivers pause
To listen to the footfalls of the Evening.

Covered in her long tresses
Having drunk the redness of the setting sun
The golden face of Evening is invisible.
If the rogue Moon had cast an eye upon the Evening,
Even He would have refused to mount the night.

Hidden among long tresses,
Evening's beautiful face
Within the grey veil
No one can see.

(translated from Dogri by Mrinal Pande and Arlene Zide)

THESE KINGS' PALACES, ARE THEY YOURS?

I've been thrown out of my house
The light of my eyes snatched away
Those who blinded me and threw me here
Took my sapling and uprooted it from my garden
My young sapling, which had not even
Borne its clusters of new blossoms.
My beloved had not even gone very far off
When they chopped off its trembling branches.
Those sickles, those hatchets, are they yours?

                These kings' palaces, are they yours?

These high walls touch the skies
The palace opulent with riches and treasures
These bricks, their vibrant crimson seems so pleasant,
But brings back to us the memory of our blood.
This is where rivers of sweat flowed from our bodies
This is where our shoulders unloaded the rafters
Those who stood in the sun and raised these walls
Are these, their palaces, yours?

                These kings' palaces, are they yours?

Even to deaf ears, the cannon spoke
I am twelve o'clock again, today
This is the time for the rising of my moon
But there was no sound of footsteps in the lanes
Not even of my own feet
That used to run to greet my man
Now I cannot stand to hear
Even the familiar sound of my beloved's voice.
Those iron chains that encircled him,
And took him from me, when he was halfway to our door
Are they yours?

                These kings' palaces, are they yours?

Those who brightened their dark nights,
Lit lamps filled with our blood.

In Their Own Voice

The moonlight clasps the moon close to itself
She watches us from afar and mocks us.
When fireworks are let loose through the sky
The stars inside us are extinguished.
Are those beautiful Diwali lamps at which our tiny children
        gape like savages, yours?

                These kings' palaces, are they yours?

It was we who dug, manured and planted the flowerbeds,
It was we who watered them in the burning sun,
We who drank from dirty moats surrounding the mud huts
My beloved got angry
Seeing the exhaustion on my dried-up face.
When they flowered
Our hearts flowered too,
And when they budded, we lit Diwali lamps in
celebration.
But somebody's anger-filled eyes demanded of our eyes
These beautiful flowerbeds, are they yours?

                These kings' palaces, are they yours?

He who already belonged to someone,
She who was given away at a tender age,
One look at her and the eyes blossomed with pleasure,
She in whose memory days merge with the night
He whose name is used by girls for teasing her,
They who have already vowed all vows,
Their souls, are they yours?

                These kings' palaces, are they yours?

        (translated from Dogri by Mrinal Pande and Arlene Zide)

MALAVIKA RAJBANS SANGHVI

GROWING OLD

My head on your lap,
You stroke my hair,
But I know you're searching for whites.
How quaint, how cute to go grey
At twenty-five, each day like needles
They push out my youth. I wear
My hair like a crown. And
Everything that must sag, sags.
Soft flesh that's known no pain
Hard to tap beneath for bone, nothing
Can reach within.
Only the mind ticks away like a bomb.

We're each dying at the same rate
One day at a time. Yet poised
On stilettos I do my balancing act.
Child-woman, pre-pubescent girl. Also
Wise old owl, lugging my bloated
Ulcer-ridden body. Scanning a mirror
I see only waste ahead and beyond.
The body's brief promise
Lets us all down.

INDIRA SANT

ALONE

She's alone.—
She earns her own living.
No matter then what she's like. Big or small,
married or single. Poor or rich.
In the end she's alone.—
Her door, open. Inside there's chatter—
the flies of meddlesome questions humming all over,
inside, outside—who's there, what's happening,
what's it all about? An idle curiosity.—
Her door, shut. The arrows of questions
stuck on the door, restless. Engrossed in gossip,
knotting up the mind.—
She goes out by herself—all dressed up,
mind at ease. But after her
a barrage of questions—where's she going,
who's she visiting, why's she going there?
A ferment of inquisitiveness.
Her accomplishment, all her own—
promotion, salary increase, successful examination.
The heads of those questions lowered in shame.
Disappointed—vicious.
How did she get it, who did her a favour,
what did she give in return?—
A lock on her door. All the questions
left with a bitter taste.
Eager to call a condolence meeting.—
Questions questions questions—always with her.
These questions
raised by her mothers and sisters—
her companions here today—there tomorrow.
Is she all alone?—How come? Who's she?
Where's she from? Why's she alone?
And. And—

(translated from Marathi by Vinay Dharwadker)

SARVAMANGALA

DOLL

I had a lovely doll
when I was small.

She would squeak
when you made her bow,
smile with her eyes
when straight
and sleep without a sound
on her back.

A head of curly hair,
lips of coral. A glance
of crystal.
Roses in her cheeks.
Tiny mouth, nose, ears.
and tiny feet.
Jhumkis in her ears.
A blue dress with white dots.

The doll was always in my lap
or at my waist.

When a sister was born,
I was afraid she would claim
my doll.
So I put my life into the doll,
put the doll in a rosewood box
grandmother had given me,
locked it tight, and hid the key

Months rolled away.
Years.
I finished college
Took a job.
Looking for a certificate,
I opened the box with the rusty key.

In Their Own Voice

Little moths
flew in my face.
The doll's clothes were rags.
Holes instead of nose, eyes,
and ears.
She had no mouth at all.
When I picked her up,
her hair and cotton stuffing
fell in wisps.
Her hands were stumps.

I didn't have the heart
to throw her out.
I took out my papers,
left the doll in the box
and locked it.

In my sleep
the doll in the box laughs
Tempts me
to open it.

(translated from Kannada by A. K. Ramanujan)

YASHODHARA SATHE

In one night, that body, every pore afire
lent its arms
just enough for a touch.
These touches never reached
the inner moth.
When her constant quivering
reaches your eyes
then
there will be no more nights.

(translated from Marathi by Asha Mundlay and Arlene Zide)

PRATIBHA SATPATHY

INSECT

I don't accept my doom.
The fire is before me
Its brightness, its light
Beautiful,
Mesmerizing.
Who can overcome its lure?

Like tiny raindrops
These two wings of mine
Glisten
Quivering, set to fly.
My eager self
Hurries after light,
Leaps over darkness
Leaps over the Earth;
Is washed away
In the flood of emotion.
Where does it go?

Spellbound
Posed in the midst of an embrace,
My body
Which lives from moment to moment,
My brief life
That flaps its restless wings,
My lifesbreath
Thriving
On the thirst for light,
Rushes forward.
All counsel proven false.

Why should I
Stay sunk in darkness.
For what?
Why such counsel?
All for the brief span of a day?

In Their Own Voice

No, not even one day.
Let the Now—
This single moment
Be my life.

I know my terrible fate;
I also know, My Creator
Your harsh laws.
I have incised them
On the carapace of my body.

Still
I don't accept my doom
I don't.

(translated from Oriya by the author and Arlene Zide)

THE FALKLANDS

In the water that eyes cannot reach
A slice of green full of life
In the branches thick with leaves
The restful nest,
Innocent leaves dancing in the breeze,
Reverberating with the chatter of young birds
Mankind's eternal land
The Falklands . . .
Where did all this fire come from?
From where the stretching of these pointed claws?
These sharp teeth?
Now there is only black smoke
Only blood—
Is this the blind vulture's greed?
His ruthless pride?

Say, you who ordains the fate of this world
Look,

In Their Own Voice

At all this charred green
This ravaged, bleeding nest
Look,
How, stretching out his wings
The bloodthirsty, blind vulture within you
Has blotted out the entire sky.

(translated from Oriya by J. P. Das and Arlene Zide)

SAVITHRI

DACOITS

When the teacher said:
    I'll get you married off
    if you don't recite the lesson
I was afraid.

When my brother said:
    My 'husband' is my boss
    who never grants me leave
    even when I need it most
I grew suspicious.

When the neighbours said:
    But, he's a man, a 'maharaja'
    so what could he be missing?
I understood.

That marriage is a huge punishment,
<u>that a husband</u> gobbles up your freedom,
and that half the population
that we nourished at the breast
divides
and rules.

(translated from Telegu by C. Rama Rao and Arlene Zide)

NILIMA SEN-GANGOPADHYAY

FISSION

>We will obey
>the rule of the atom
>depart
>beyond the planets

(O excruciating ache
give them   greenfield
dovecall   brookwater
dawnlight)

>we will leave behind
>flower bird grain river
>we have seen its face, the
>un born
>un arrived
>do not call us back

(O airpoison burns eyes   blood
boils to gas
hearts flail   lungs drown
in fluid)

>howmuchlonger?

>>after the explosion
>>we will wake live again
>>again incantate life

(O they don't know
ownself   futuredark
atomseed in earthvein
   illplanet
pulling them
to wreckage)

(translated from Bengali by Chitra Banerjee Divakaruni)

MALLIKA SENGUPTA

THE CARRIERS OF FIRE

India had no horses then. They came
Kicking up the dust of the Caucasus,
Bearing on their backs the carriers of fire—
Men from a terrible, handsome warrior clan.

Handsome men, but no such women came.
I'm the daughter of Indus, soil, water and grass.
If they desire me, let anything transpire.
I'm a trampled star. Even warriors are men.

Seeing that the coppery sky on dark skin
Looks so bright, the riders of horses put fire
In the womb; the warrior god Kartik* was sired.

Not only brave warriors, the blood mingling in
My womb. They are my husband, children, brothers
From a dry land, become the offspring of rivers.

* the warrior-god of Hindu mythology, son of Shiva (the 'destroyer' aspect of the divine triad) and his consort Durga, revered for her slaying of the demon Ravana in battle

(translated from Bengali by Paramita Banerjee and Carolyne Wright)

HOME

Get the bamboo poles ready before intercourse,
A home must be erected.
My son I'll carry on my back.
The Drishadbati River flows there still—
Silt, new vegetation.

Oh Unmoving Father—bless us so that this winter
We don't set out again as nomads.

(translated from Bengali by Paramita Banerjee and Carolyne Wright)

In Their Own Voice

ROBOT

A satellite is eclipsing the earth.
A robot lies alone on its sickbed.
Its eyes are exactly human. Against its rib
A lighted button pulses on and off.

The robot lies alone under a blue sky.
It doesn't want a cure; it wants to be human.
Unreasonable society wants a robot-victory.
INSAT 1B eclipses the earth.

The chief wants a satellite-cure.
The republic wants a society of robots.
The Way of the Robot will liberate the earth.
A gecko laughs from behind the canvas.

Being Indian, the robot will be born again,
emerging through the alleyways of the human womb.
Ten p.m.: the satellite is sighted.
Ten p.m.: the robot's pulse ceases.

(translated from Bengali by Chitra Banerjee Divakaruni)

RAJEE SETH

BUNGALOW ON THE MOUNTAIN

An old man
The baggage of life's experience tucked under his arm
Sleeping, waking
When will they all come?
And listen to what happened over this rough winter
When no one else was here.
What happened in Winter, in Spring
When the koel sang.
How the valley slept, undraped
How it slept dressed in snow
How the flowerbeds shivered with the cold,
The baby plants huddled down
How the smug lightning descended from the sky
And challenged the green earth.
How the red terraces switched their loyalties to white.

They came running
Trampling the valley underfoot
Viewing the whole scene from behind a pane of glass
Transistor/Filmsongs
Bags of popcorn/Eggshells
Caps from coca-cola bottles,
Old embroidered carpets hanging on the cottage walls
Jazz/Rock/poptunes/an omelette/chicken/rum
Tongues of flame flickering in the fireplace
The clatter of dishes
Cold water
The dirtied dishes in the old man's trembling hands,
What warped intelligence!
Why don't they want to know
What happened to the sky/to the earth/and to the trees

To the flowers, to the butterflies
All those days
When all of them
Were not here.

(translated from Hindi by Aruna Sitesh and Arlene Zide)

In Their Own Voice

MY SISTERS

You are busy
Sharpening your weapons
To unman the men
I acquiesce in my womanhood
Totally.
Totally.

I clean up the sooty walls of my hearth
And caress the sides of my womb
I feed the tender mouths
Of tiny infants
With live embers
Of a revolution.

(translated from Hindi by Lakshmi Kannan)

RITA SHAHANI

AND THE KNITTING GOES ON

Here I am knitting a sweater
Minute to minute, weaving thoughts
and the knitting goes on . . .

Four knit, four purl
Two rows forward
Not going back
The war trumpets below
and the weaving goes on.

Purl, knit, wool over, knit two
Knit two together, knit two.
the needles click, the wool speeds
The race-course comes to life
The horses running
and the weaving goes on.

Loop over loop
The sweater takes shape
Keep in step and
The form will emerge
So reason says
and the weaving goes on.

Stitch + stitch = a Pashmina shawl
Brick + brick = a home
Word + word = a poem
Note + note = a melody
the knitting goes on.

(translated from Sindhi by the author)

SHAKUNTALA DEVI

MAGICIAN

My noon blazed as in the blistering month of *Baisakh*
How damp it was how warm
> Like a writhing fish near the banks
> I opened my spider eyes and peered from
> > The distant window.

The heat, the blazing sun.
Suddenly silent on the lonely island.
The morning's multi-coloured butterflies
Fluttered about, laughing
Chanting hymns of sacred moments.

> When noon arrived they became drowsy,
> Shrunk with fear,
> Seeing me in this new guise.

> A flower said, how do you feel
> And dropped to the ground
> This life took on new form
> Midday turned to afternoon, then evening
> Opened up the net
> And one by one, threw away the fish.

From my window, the furrow of memory lengthened
The sun departing in the sky, the half-light half-shadow
    of the world
I became trapped in my own amazement.

(translated from Oriya by J. P. Das and Arlene Zide)

SHAFIQ FATIMA SHEIRA

THE CITY OF THE VOICE

The tulip bud with a song on its lips
Had sent forth its fragrance in these very surroundings
Wrapped in a leaf, removing a petal
Its nectar filled a season's cask
With lingering golden sunshine.

An entire season was needed to bend the bough, scatter petals
Create dense shade, garden after garden,
And ponds, brimming over with water.
Like gusts of wind, all paths remain forever frantic
All ages past and future times
All hamlets new, deserted towns
Refugees, inhabitants forever recounting old tales
Without end.

Generation after generation sipping darkness.
There lie those sole-hardening roads of today
Their stoniness slowly swallowing the totality of being.
Till the eyes cease moving, tears freeze.

When in loneliness
The shadow of a branch slides like a snake,
Every sound has in its unseen hand
A knife, gleaming off and on.
Then who appears?
A hand placed gently on the shoulder?
Is it Khusro's* song?
A moment the union of eons, of lives and dreams—
Bursts forth like a cascade out of the stones?
These eyes of mine can open in what far away times
Waters of this shade, cool and rich with the sweet fragrance of
your clay jar?

---

* **Ameer Khusro**, the 14th c. poet, mystic and musician of Delhi who made many innovations in Hindustani music, was the chief disciple of the Sufi saint, Nizamuddin Aulia. Nizamuddin said that on the morning of creation when God had asked the souls, 'Am I not your Lord?,' each soul heard these words in various different ragas. Nizamuddin Aulia heard it in the raga *Purvi*.

In Their Own Voice

Balm for inner wounds—
My eyes can open in what far away times!
All is just as if it were real—
People, white-washed dwellings, earth and sky—
In these very surroundings
There had descended once
The City of the Voice.

That city was a lamp of time.
It burned here in the storm of time
Parts of its ramparts and forts have vanished,
Continue to vanish.
Encampments too.

The heritage of eons,
Purvi, the raga of the East,
The familiar mode,
The season of mustard flowers
Drenched in a soft spring warmth
Remain.

The minstrels, wandering
Stop for a moment and wonder about me,
Who is this poet?
Which ocean raised this cloud—
What perilous distances it traversed
To reach this valley and find the hour to
Shower its rains.

(*translated from Urdu by Qurratulain Hyder and Arlene Zide*)

In Their Own Voice

THE PLAY OF THE SEASONS (ELLORA)

The season comes, the season goes,
We wake with every season, turn over on our side, sleep again.
Roses, showers, the wordless wonderment of childhood
Shining cloud-boats, water-plains,
Shadow islands of green
Clear, happy bumble-bee eyes,
Laughter-fountains,
Then the dust-smoke curtain of change.
The play of the seasons.

Hidden from one's eyes
The revolving heart, astonished.
Lost in an unknown frost,
Naked full-moon night, sheer, liquid.
A haunted silence dissolving in ruins.
One day I found my pen seemed to have dissolved too!

Sheira! Sheira! perhaps a bird called.
Those winding paths inside the half-dark caves
Brought forth reverberating waves of sound
Brought them out into the hot sun.
Sparkling beneath the sun,
The waterfall,
Its incessant roar,
The noise of the flying spray,
Cool, glittering, mercurial
Spilling over,
Mirror for the sun's rays.

Stone figures, their
Stone silence—my own life.
Then, a sound of splinters
Perhaps it was a glass—my own heart.
Ungrateful, ungrateful—
Whispers of the busy, angry wind.
Ungrateful, your treasures of blossoms and fruit—
Who sent them from the high boughs, you?
Just you?

Ungrateful! The whispers and conversation went on.
How many seasons changed. How many destinies and scripts.
Their appearance and disappearance contained in our rise and fall.
But even while making our exit we continued to proclaim
>   We were the best.
And smiled!

How it all seems a dream.
Deep waters, the end of memory.
Liquid, a star-song grows from a dusty courtyard,
The reason for living.
Whose is it?
Not mine. Yet it seems so much my own.
Marvelling at it, I do not recall the business of 'us' and 'you'
What feeling is this?
Whom to ask?
And what is this feeling's name?

>   (translated from Urdu by Qurratulain Hyder and Arlene Zide)

SHANTA SHELKE

ON MY WAY BACK

On these many roads I walked and
broke myself, spilled myself, spread myself all over.
Now, on my way back again
I look for the many scattered
fragments of myself,
I try to piece together one unbroken whole.
The darkness grows around me.

(translated from Marathi by Asha Mundlay and Arlene Zide)

IF YOU LOOK AT IT LIKE THAT

If you look at it like that
Every once in a while, there are so many
Shapes of nothingness
In this enduring relationship of ours.
Suddenly, on the glowing dazzle of these paths
Lurk dark corners
Loom difficult climbs and slopes
And treacherous, fatal curves.

We've come this far, safe and sound, despite this.
Call it just a little, or you can call this a lot
Only the eyes have become wary, listless
Footsteps wiser.
And new paths gradually unfolding before us
Write themselves on our palms, mine and yours.

(translated from Marathi by Asha Mundlay and Arlene Zide)

SHREE DEVI

ON A SHIKAR
For Nissim Ezekiel

Even the person who says he isn't afraid of anything
Feels his bones collapse
In the midst of an Indian jungle,
Where brown trunks loom high
And a few gold rays pierce the hypodermic density.
Every rustle all but stops the heart
(But never actually does,
Death being nearly always unexpected).
It's rather nice to see two eyes gleaming in the pitchiness
And not know what type of body they may belong to.
They may even belong to nobody.
Usually the most dangerous kind
Slant upwards
Waiting to pounce on humanity.
Belonging of course to such creatures as
Panthers, leopards or the Chinese.

One longs to rest, but flora thickens what with health, home, etc.
You must keep standing or try
Headstands like a Yogi's if the feet get weary—
While the mind conjures up visions of a double bed,
Eager man and all. He may even be muscular:
Things depend on how perfect the imagination is.
Just as some Elizabethans saw not the 'Wooden O' but
Gasped at moving Birnam greens.
While others kept thinking in the midst of her best speeches
That Juliet's breasts were only padding.

But one always comes to a stream,
Tries to sip philosophy but being thirsty
Gulps muddy water.
Embarrassed to see two elephants mating. Yet oddly excited.
Is God as great as we make Him out to be?
At times I feel He's wholly human.
He kept insisting he was a virgin—maybe he was.

You don't have to insist on anything at all.
Nobody's really interested.

LAST AT NIGHT AT 3 A.M.

Tiptoeing tensely towards suicide
I stumbled on rusted religion,
The clatter resurrecting my Convent girlhood
Scrubbed with soap...

Moving within the dark walls of nun's skirts,
I made a dash for freedom,
'No treacle for tea,' said Mother Bernard,
Slapping my pride.

I escaped anyway,
Climbing barefoot transparent gates of the imagination
And returning with calloused feet.

My playmate on the other end of the see-saw, fell.
Only when I saw the cobwebs on her tooth-brush
Did I envy her.

All I asked him for was the gift of pride.
Searching for it, I saw him seated on our bed,
Leaning over someone.

BEHEROZE F. SHROFF

MOTHER

Sucked into currents
of married life at nineteen,
your youth and energy were harnessed
to serve a mother-in-law's sick-bed.

Husband, pushed into background,
the family machine took over.
Speculating the promise
of the bride's fruitful womb,
they turned uneager
after the yield of three years:
'Only daughters?'

They required your
production unit
to function again;
as aids prescribed prayers,
gave holy water from Babas
and charms from Gurus.

Like a bucket of water
scraped out of a low-laying well,
a son was obtained from you,
claimed from birth by each aunt, uncle
to be the product of *their* holy effort.

The father made hero
was congratulated, praised, feted.

The mother was given
tips on child-rearing.

BRIDGE AND TEA PARTY

'My daughter,' says Mrs Shah
'is S.S.C. pass, high Second Class,
Headgirl in school, very interested
in life; we encourage it—pictures
parties shopping visiting
active child.'

'My Ayesha did her Cambridge abroad,
scholarship from British Council
she'll be settling in England or
the U.S. on a green card.'

'My Renu is very popular
they call her Ren at college,
her name came in the papers
you know—students' revolt.'

'I'll call Bunty
darling sing what
teacher taught you
sing near aunty.'

MELANIE SILGARDO

DORIS

Gently touch the earth.
It locks your feet.
It locks your feeble heart
that's losing time.
No one calls you Doris any more.

For the first time
the firm earth trembles.
It opened and swallowed them
one by one. The ones you went
to school with, who later
served their husbands as you did.
Early mother, late widow.

Your sons have long dispersed
your daughters drag their feet.
You are no longer sure.
That early confidence and
stern hold on our ears
has broken into fear.
Fear of the dark
and fear that you might
wet your bed
and we'd hear about it.

No one calls you Doris any more
because they are dead.
Alive, are your granddaughters
and grandsons
pursuing the same ancient plague.
You would warn them,
but only brittle age rolls off your tongue.

ILA RANI SINGH

MISFIT

A complete misfit everywhere
Pond, I come to you
To have a dip
Keep on floating
In your everflowing stream of time
Plunge
My dried and withered body and mind
In your natural freshness.

I feel like eating
Coarse red *dasaria* rice,
Fresh fish from the pond
Adauri and *janera* roti*
Like my aunty makes.
I want to play pretending games like *dom kach*
On a full-moon night
And, on every tree of the village
Carve my name—
That nickname, Treasure, you once gave me
Carved into the tree.
Who can erase it?
Who can steal it?

---
* fried dumplings made from soaked urad dal flour and ash gourd

(translated from Maithili by Anjani K. Sinha and Arlene Zide

KABITA SINHA

CURSE

Look now, the entire forest has gone dead
    as wood in this room,
In that polished four-poster bed   In that
    nocturnal chair!
You are sitting on a tree's tomb.
And on the table, the stony-eyed cockatoo
Is a dead bird hunched on a dead branch.
And you are absorbing their curses daily!

Because you alone have thrashed the whole forest
    to death.

This chunk of wood once gave forth living flowers;
Inside the myriad solid buds
Thick, continuous life poured out.

Your fancy bedstead won't be decked with flowers now.
The pillow's cotton stuffing hankers for revenge.
It will throw its damning silken cobwebs
    into your dreams.

The disembodied forest will breathe into you,
And among all this wood you will be
Slowly turned to wood.

The life force will drain out of your five senses.

(translated by Enakshi Chatterjee and Carolyne Wright)

EVE SPEAKS TO GOD

I was first
to know
that which rises
is the other side
of that which falls

In your creation
what is light
is also dark
I was first
to know

To obey
or not obey
weighs the same
I was first
to know

First to finger
the knowledge tree,
to bite into
the red apple
I was first

I was first
to divide
heaven and hell
with a fig leaf,
shame and
shamelessness

I was first
to water the stem
of this pleasure-body
with pain
first to know
like you
we too
can fashion dolls,
to see
your face
in my newborn's
I was first

I was first
to know
grief and joy

In Their Own Voice

sin and goodness
mingled
makes living
unique

I was first
to break
the golden chains
of unmixed ease
no puppet
to your
fisted strings
like
low Adam

I was the first
rebel
on your earth
I was first

My love
my slave
I was first
first woman
first exile
fallen
banished

first to know
this human life
is higher
than heaven
higher than
heaven

I was first
to know

(translated from Bengali by Chitra Banerjee Divakaruni)

SUGATHAKUMARI

THE RAIN AT NIGHT

The rain-at-night
Meaninglessly weeping,
laughing, sobbing
muttering without stop
Sitting huddled up
like some young madwoman,
shaking out its long hair—

The rain-at-night
Like a drawn-out sob
slowly entering this hospital room
An ice-cold finger
floating in
touches you—
Sad daughter of this dark night

The rain-at-night.
Wincing with a start of pain,
the sharp-edged cries,
a mother's sudden anguished wail.
On my sickbed, tossing from side to side,
I sob
through darkness.
Like beloved friends and relatives
consoling me with their gentle words
the night-rain comes.

I clap my hands over my ears.
Someone says:
> You can cut off a diseased limb
> But what about a poor, diseased mind?

The rain-at-night,
in those long-ago nights of my married life
made me laugh, spread a thrill of joy along the skin
lulled me to sleep with a delight

greater than even the white moonlight could bestow—
Witness to my love.

The rain-at-night.
Now on this hot sickbed of mine
in the sleepless hours,
alone in darkness
forgetting even to weep,
I toss about,
harden into stone.

Rain-at-night,
Witness to my sorrow.
Oh! Rain-at-night, I understand
your music, melting with grief
your pity,
your suppressed anger,
your stealing about at night,
your lonely sobbing.
And when the morning comes,
I understand your hurry,
and your play-acting,
why you freshen up your face, and laugh.

Friend, you know, don't you
why I understand all this?
Because, like you, I too
am like the rain-at-night.

(translated from Malayalam by the author, Hrdayakumari and Arlene Zide)

SUKRITA

A BORROWED EXISTENCE

The still-born world
trembles out of its stillness
when he and she and it
(each one my own thought)
pulsate their way out of me

I too wriggle from some mind

Each one of us
is merely someone's thought
and each thought
merely a deserter
of God.

THILAKAVATHI

WOMAN, THIS, TOO, IS A WOUND TO BE PROUD OF

there's an unfair animal
fighting on the battleground
a real coward
a mean thing
he touched your body
and just for *that*, woman,
you'd dare to give up your life?

stand up, girl
stand up straight
knit your brow
think long
hiss
and rise in anger
woman, be brave

think a little
you
are a field that yields heroism
strengthen
neither the enemy's hand
nor his desire
by committing suicide

don't pour *ghee* into a fire
to put it out
don't build a high dam
with water
to stop a flood

if he's wounded in battle
he thinks it's something to be proud of
and turns haughty
your brother
beats his chest
and you?

In Their Own Voice

if the enemy's hand
touches your body
you go crazy
and climb on a pyre
doesn't your act lend speed
to this man who wants to ruin you?

that man who's buried
in the muck along with you
he'll mistake the crud that falls in on his body
for sandalpaste
and he'll take his pleasure

if you are subjected to violence
all by yourself
you'll lose your life
he
will enter the fire
together with you
and will return a hero
but you
will burn to ash in the flames

woman
about that thing called chastity
be clear-headed
all of the laws
in every age
are customs that change

once upon a time
because it tripped us
even a stone was hanged

now
even a jerk
a serial murderer
will get a lease on life
thanks to a psychiatrist

In Their Own Voice

even so, woman,
from the second century
to the twenty-first
the chains
that bind you
are not broken
why?
o flame that burns for all of eternity
on the battleground of life
how can this filth touch you?

o unequalled wealth
of the motherland that brought you forth
all this violence
that has been poured down upon you
is just dust in fire

rise
take off those bangles
brandish a sword
burn like fire
swell upward
spin like a whirlwind
rise

(translated from Tamil by Martha Ann Selby and K. Paramasivam)

MANJIT TIWANA

HUSBAND

A husband is a hungry wolf
Who shields you from all other wolves
But himself . . .

Fixing you between his jaws
He boasts:
>'See, how safe you are!
>I don't devour you' . . .

A husband is a hungry wolf
Who shields you from all other wolves
But himself . . .

A machine
He fits in all your spare parts,
Weeding out every hair on the body of your existence.
Questions:
>'Who the hell are you?'
Instantly, like Red Riding Hood
You want to run away
But like a lightning flash he catches you.
Bewildered, you search desperately for yourself.

A husband is a hungry wolf
Who saves you from all other wolves
But ultimately
Devours you.

(translated from Punjabi by the author and edited by Arlene Zide)

SUNANDA TRIPATHY

THE TRYST

When the whole city is asleep
I take off my anklets
and come into your room
On soft, stolen steps.

You lie there, unmoving,
on the disordered bed,
books strewn all around.
In their midst, alone, you lie asleep,
a smile of some strange contentment
on your sleeping face.
I sit quietly by the bed,
smooth your dishevelled hair,
then, bend down and with my sharp nails
tear open your chest,
and with both my hands scoop out
a fistful of pulsating soft pink flesh.

I am spellbound by the odour of that flesh
I hold it to my breast.
For a moment,
The word and the silence become one,
then, sky and earth—
they become one.

Before you wake
I put it back in place,
caress your open chest.
The wound fills up in a moment
As if nothing had happened.
As before, you go on sleeping
I walk, quietly, from your room.

(translated from Oriya by J. P. Das and Arlene Zide)

In Their Own Voice

POEM IN MOTION

There is some ash/some blood
Sticking to the wings
A dove flies
Around a ring of fire.

The people there
Mill around
Dressed in paper clothes.

Here youth falls
With the winter leaves
While someone signs a deed of compromise,
Reading the marks
Beneath someone's lowcut neckline,
Another runs off.
Here youth falls with the winter leaves.

At the muffled cry
Of the ruined walls
The deep slumber
Of winter nights shatters.

The man on the street
Drags you to his alley
Where last night someone
Burnt down his hut.

While I was away
Time slipped under the door
A sealed envelope
I am afraid of opening.

(translated from Oriya by J. P. Das and Arlene Zide)

SA. USHA

TO MOTHER

Mother, don't, please don't,
don't cut off the sunlight
with your sari spread across the sky
blanching life's green leaves.

Don't say: you're seventeen already,
    don't flash your sari in the street,
    don't make eyes at passers-by,
    don't be a tomboy riding the winds

Don't play that tune again
what your mother
her mother and her mother
had played on the snake charmer's flute
into the ears of nitwits like me.
I'm just spreading my hood.
I'll sink my fangs in someone
and lose my venom.
Let go, make way.

Circumambulating the holy plant
in the yard, making rangoli designs
to see heaven, turning up dead
without light and air,
for god's sake, I can't do it.
Breaking out of the dam
you've built, swelling
in a thunderstorm,
roaring through the land
let me live, very different
from you, Mother.
Let go, make way.

(translated from Kannada by A. K. Ramanujan)

VAIDEHI
(JANAKI SRINIVASAMURTHY)

GIRL IN THE KITCHEN

Like other things
they say a kitchen too
means many things
but for this girl—
this kitchen is her house
this that and every house
even the house of burial

Just as every creature
has a stomach
every house has a kitchen
I don't know whose plan it is
no windows no doors
not even a chimney for the smoke
not even a hole somewhere—
she longs for one.

As she cooks
the birds outside
the noise of playing children
buses cars autorickshaws running
into the distance
even to the seashore
but she ignores them
as she grinds the spices
renunciation comes easy, doesn't it,
when you have nothing?

Yet sometimes if she hears
the airplane in the sky
the plane! the plane! she cries
from where she is
after all what trips can she take
while she is with salt and tamarind?
the twenty-first century?

will you take me with you?
the sound in the sky
melts away
v e r y   s l o w l y

This B.C. girl in the kitchen
blows *foo foo* into the fire
and sings
maybe there's surely someone
up there in the plane
a gentleman in make-up and costume
as surely as all creatures are born
to steal and to rule

Maybe the flying chariot
will flap its wings
break through the roof
let down a ladder
lift me up as I peel potatoes
and make me the chief queen

O Rama, Rama! carrying me
to Lanka or to Ayodhya?
old names and places
heard many times before
now what about worlds
no one has heard of?
fly to those worlds
I command you

and so on—
she weaves songs this girl
her ears open to the sounds in the sky
breaking the stalks of green chillies
her lifetime getting spent drop by drop

(translated from Kannada by A. K. Ramanujan)

ARCHANA VERMA

MAN

Water on a slope
will run downhill, they said
with an air of finality.
That is, if water is water.

They didn't say: soil on a slope
if it's really soil
will soak up water.
That a green carpet of grass
will sprout, covering the slope. It
may lie covering the slope, but
will turn its face skywards.
That is, if grass is really grass.

We're all standing on a slope. This
was the topic of discussion that evening. Water
can only flow downwards. This
was their conclusion. Trees
were not discussed at all. They may spring up
at the bottom of the slope, but
they grow upwards. The bigger
they grow, the more easily
they are uprooted. That is, if trees
Are really trees.

But the water
was not water. And the grass
wasn't grass either. Or trees,
trees.

But the topic wasn't water or grass, or trees.
It was man, about him
no one
said a word.

(translated from Hindi by Aruna Sitesh and Arlene Zide)

In Their Own Voice

KITE

An unsolved question
In these two eyes
And behind this question
A lack of faith
They pierce my consciousness

The way a huge-winged kite
Riding the wind
In straight and steady flight
Cuts across the sky.

(translated from Hindi by Aruna Sitesh and Arlene Zide)

SHEFALIKA VERMA

MY VILLAGE

Whenever I come back to my village
The village and only the village sits in my mind
On the edge of the wide *makana* leaf
In the tossing of the *karmi* vines
Swaying at the border of the moonlit night
In the midst of endless natural beauty.

Sitting here
On the banks of a canal
I sing in the midst of struggle
A song of life
And weave a honeyed dream.

My village
In the monsoon, drenched
In summer, bathed in the heat of the sun
Huddled up in winter.
During the Panchayat elections,
Turning over on its side.

Squabbling and bickering
In harmony and balance,
Blossoming and ripening
My village.
There on the banks of the river Koshi
Always before my eyes.
Like the golden jasmine of my dreams.

The bird of Time flies off
And
What remains in memory,
Its colours changing like the sky,
Biting into the *makana* leaf,
Is the snake,
Slithering among the *karmi* leaves.

(translated from Maithili by Anjani K. Sinha and Arlene Zide)

VIMALA

KITCHEN

This kitchen: how wonderful,
wafting aromas,
how it makes mouths water!
Like an open shop of sweets.

It breathes spices,
incense from the puja room,
wakes in the morning
to the noise of churning butter,
of vessels being scrubbed.

The earthen oven gets a fresh mudwash,
decks herself for the burning
from the small change
in the box of spices and seasonings.

We bought ourselves sweets,
played house, played at being cooks
with jaggery and lentils.
It was a magic world.
The kitchen snared my childhood,
remained a spell, a passion.

Wisps of childhood shadows lifted,
it's no longer a playground.
They taught me kitchenness here,
my shaping started here.
Mother, Grandmother, all the mothers
in the house, they say,
learned womanhood here.

Our kitchen now is a graveyard
with corpses of all kinds,
tins, dishes, sacks.
It hangs there in the smoke,
clouds from damp firewood.

Fears, despair, silence lurking there,
Mother floats like a spirit,
she looks like the morning kitchen herself.
Her eyes ran out of tears long ago.
Her hands are worn out with endless scrubbing.
Look, she doesn't have hands anymore.

She looks like a ladle, a pan, a bowl,
a piece of kitchen bric-a-brac.
She sometimes looks like a flaming oven,
sometimes she lurks like a trapped tigress.
Restless, she paces the kitchen floor,
bangs pots and pans.

How easily, they say, with a flick of the ladle
the cooking gets done.
No one comes this way, except
to eat.
My mother is empress of this kitchen empire,
but the name on the pots and pans is my father's.

Fortunately, they said, I fell into a good kitchen:
gas stove, grinder, sink and tiles.
I make cakes and puddings,
not old-fashioned things like my mother.
Still the name on everything is my husband's.

My kitchen wakes
to the whirr of the electric grinder,
the hiss of the pressure cooker.
I move like my modern kitchen,
a wind-up toy.
My kitchen is like a workshop,
even a butcher's shop with its babble.

Washing what has been washed endlessly,
cooking and serving, cooking and serving,
scrubbing and washing,
there's a kitchen even in my dreams,
the smell of spices even in the jasmine,
damn this kitchen!

In Their Own Voice

Inhuman, it sucks our blood, robs us
of hope and dream,
a demon, a vulture
eating into us bit by bit all our lives.
Kitchen culture. Kitchen talk.
Reduced to kitchen maids and cooks.

Let's smash these kitchens
for making ladle-wielding our ultimate duty.
No more names on kitchen things.
Let's uproot these separate stoves.
Our children are about to enter
these lonely kitchens.
Come, for their sake,
let us demolish
these kitchens, now!

*(translated from Telugu by V. V. B. Rama Rao, edited by Arlene Zide
and A. K. Ramanujan)*

NOTES ON AUTHORS AND TRANSLATORS

Shanta Acharya b. 1953, Cuttack, Orissa. MA in English from Ravenshaw College, in 1974, where she taught before going to Oxford in 1979, D.Phil., English, 1983; Harvard Visiting Scholar. Her poetry has appeared in publications in India, UK and the USA. She now lives in London.

Indrani Aikath-Gyaltsen b. 1952. She was schooled in Sacred Heart Convent, Jamshedpur and later went to Barnard College, New York. A tea-planter's wife, she has one son and lives in Darjeeling. Her novels have been published by Penguin India and her first collection of poems, *The First Jacaranda*, was published in 1985.

Meena Alexander b. 1951, Allahabad. She is from Kerala; her poetry includes *Stone Roots* (1980), *House of A Thousand Doors* (1988), *The Storm* (1989) and *Night-Scene, the Garden* (1992). At present she lives and works in New York City, where she teaches at Hunter College and the Graduate Centre (CUNY).

Malika Amar Shaikh b. 1956, Bombay. She has published one book of poems, *Valu Cha Priyakar* (1979) and an autobiography (1984). Her new collection of poems, *Mahanagar* (Megalopolis) is slated for publication soon. An editor of *Nantar*, she has written three one-act plays and two novels as well.

Bala b. 1966, Madras. An artist and painter, she is currently working on experimental poetry and short stories. She resides in Madras, where she was born and brought up.

Balamani Amma born in Kerala. A well-respected and beloved narrative poet of Kerala, she is the mother of poet, Kamala Das.

Banaja Devi b. 1941, Puri, Orissa. With two collections of poems and three collections of short stories to her credit, she has been writing for leading magazines and newspapers in Orissa since the age of ten.

Sangjukta Bandyopadhyay b. 1958, Calcutta. Married and mothering a baby, she holds an MA in Comparative Literature, and works as a librarian. Her first book of poems is *Avidya* (1985); the second, *Basanta-Prakriti*, has just been released.

Shukla Bandyopadhyay b. 1952, Pachundi, Burdwan, (West Bengal). MA, Calcutta University. She works for *Ananda Bazaar Patrika*, and as Chief Advisor to *Anubad Patrika*, working on a variety of literary translations from India and abroad. Her poems have appeared in *Desh*.

Paramita Banerjee b. 1958, Calcutta. BA, Presidency College; currently engaged in philosophical research work on *Mahabharata* women, at Jadavpur University. She has been active in political theatre groups, has published articles on theatre and women's issues, poetry in leading Calcutta literary magazines. A former editor for Orient-Longman Press. Has translated two novels from Bengali to English for Penguin India.

Hira Bansode b. 1939. An MA in Marathi, she has to her credit two collections of poetry, *Paurnima* and *Firiyad*. She is the founder and former president of the Savandini Dalit Stree Sahitya Munch and has been active in the movement to help down-trodden women air their grievances and fight for their rights.

Nirmal Prabha Bardoloi b. 1933, Sibsagar, Assam. She has a dozen volumes published including novels, short story and poetry collections. She received the Sahitya Akademi Award for her book of poems *Sudirgha Din Aru Ritu* in 1983.

Anjana Basu b. 1956, Allahabad. Started school in London. Lived in America for two years where she attended Brown University as a special student. A graduate of Calcutta University, she is a part-time journalist, a full-time advertising copywriter, and a one-time academic.

Krishna Basu b. 1947, Chandannagar, West Bengal. An MA and Ph.D. in Literature, she is a college lecturer. A regular contributor to leading Bengali magazines including *Desh*, she has published five collections of poems. She was awarded the Pratisruti Puraskar in 1981.

Ishita Bhaduri b. 1961, Calcutta. The great-granddaughter of Bengali poet Jatindra Mohan Bagchi, she herself is the author of four collections of poems. She lives in Chandernagore, West Bengal where she is an architect.

Shobha Bhagwat b. 1947, Thane, Maharashtra. MA, University of Bombay. At present she is the director of 'Balbhavan' in Pune. An editor of the PTA quarterly of Maharashtra, she is the author of two books on Parents' Education, and two translations for teachers on educational experiments.

Amrita Bharati b. 1937, Najibabad, Uttar Pradesh. Holds an MA and Ph.D. in Sanskrit from Banaras Hindu University, and has taught in several colleges. She has five collections of poems to her credit and is currently engaged in translating the poems of Sri Aurobindo. She resides in Pondicherry.

Sujata Bhatt b. 1956, Ahmedabad. She studied in the US where her family settled when she was twelve. She now lives in Germany with her poet-husband, Michael Augustin and daughter, Jennifer Meera. Her first collection of poems, *Brunizem*, has been widely acclaimed. A second collection, *Monkey Shadows*, appeared in 1992.

Manorama Mohapatra (Biswal) b. 1948, Balasore, Orissa. She has published over a dozen collections of poetry in Oriya. Professor of Oriya at Rama Devi Women's College, Bhubaneshwar. Recipient of numerous honours; known for her writings in children's literature as well as poetry.

Bratati Biswas b. 1950, West Dinajpur, West Bengal. A lecturer in Philosophy, her collection of poems, *Gupta Ghatak Nisarga* (Nature, the Secret Killer) appeared in 1984.

Chandrika (Chandrika Balan) b. 1954, Kerala. Ph.D., English, from the University of Kerala. She works in the Department of English at All Saints' College, Trivandrum. She is a fiction writer and critic in Malayalam, and a critic and translator in English.

Cantirakanti (a.k.a. Chandra Gandhi, R. Uma Maheswari) b. 1961, Edapet, South Arcot, Tamil Nadu. Two collections of poems, *Ambal Arccanai* and *Malaik Kala Maunankal*. She comes from an agricultural family of Edapet village. She has also published short stories in leading Tamil magazines.

Enakshi Chatterjee b. 1934, Calcutta. MA, English, Patna University, has translated scientific and literary works from Bengali, for the USIS book translation project, into English, the writings of contemporary Bengal novelists such as Tarasankar Bandyopadhyay, Premen Mitra and Sunil Gangopadhyay, and the work of renowned nineteenth century and modern Bengali women writers.

Margaret Chatterjee b. 1925, London. She holds an MA (Oxford) and a Ph.D. (Delhi University). She has been the Head of the Department of Philosophy, Delhi University and is the former Director, Indian Institute of Advanced Study, Simla. Her publications include five collections of poems.

Chaitali Chattopadhyay b. 1960, Calcutta. Her first collection of poetry, *Bijnapaner Meye*, appeared in 1988. In 1990, her second collection, *Debipakshe Lekha Kabita* appeared. Her poetry has appeared in *Desh* and other magazines.

Gita Chattopadhyay b. 1941, Calcutta, into an orthodox Hindu zamindar family; the first girl of her family to attend college. She lives essentially in seclusion at her 150-year-old ancestral home in Calcutta. An MA and Ph.D. from Calcutta University, her collections of poetry include: *Gouri Champa Nadi*, *Chandara*, *Sapta Diba Nishi Kalkata*, *Minanko Sopan*. Some recent poems have appeared in *Kabi O Kabita* and *Samved*, and in the recently published *Bankim Chandrer Hate Banga Itihas*.

Snehmayee Chaudhary b. 1935, Maurawan, Unnao, Uttar Pradesh MA, Ph.D. in Hindi. She has been teaching at Janaki Devi Mahavidyalaya, Delhi University since 1965. She has published four collections of poems and a volume of criticism. A collection of long poems is forthcoming.

Kirti Chaudhury b. 1935, Naeempur, Dt. Unnao, Uttar Pradesh. She has spent most of her life in cities like New Delhi and Bombay. Since 1970 she has been living in London. Part of the New Wave Experimental Poetry in Hindi during the fifties, she has two collections of poetry (*Kavitayen* and *Khule Hue Asman Ke Nice*) and a number of published short stories.

Mahuya Chaudhury b. 1967, Serampore, West Bengal. A graduate in English literature from the University of Jadavpur, she has been writing since 1986. Her poems have appeared in leading literary magazines such as *Desh*, *Parichaya*, and *Rhashanagar*.

Bahinabai Chaudhury 1880-1951. An illiterate agricultural labourer who used to sing her songs as she made them up. Luckily for posterity, her son and nephew recognized her genius and scribbled down what they could. A collection was published in 1952 and she was immediately acclaimed and recognized as a towering talent in Marathi literature. The language of her poems is regional, employing the rhythms peculiar to a particular way of life in a particular part of Maharashtra. Many of her songs and lines from them have become common currency in Marathi, in the manner of the saint-poets of earlier centuries.

Vijaya Dabbe b. 1952, Dabbe. Lecturer in Kannada at the University of Mysore. She has received state awards for her poetry and criticism; has also edited and written on older Kannada literature. Two collections of poetry, *Iruttave* (1975) and *Neeru Lohada Chinte*, (1985).

Aziz Bano Darab born in Lucknow. She received her MA in English literature from the University of Lucknow in 1949. She is a well-known modern Urdu poet.

Bijoyini Das b. 1944, Baunsiapada, Puri, Orissa. MA in Psychology. She has published seventeen books, including novels, short stories and poetry.

Jagannath Prasad Das b. 1936, Puri, Orissa. Poet, playwright, historical novelist, short story writer, and art historian, he resigned from the IAS to devote himself to full-time research and writing. His works include eight collections of poetry, five collections of short stories, four plays, a historical novel, and two scholarly books: *Puri Paintings* and *Chitra-pothi*.

Jyotsna Das b. 1958, Berhampur, Orissa. MA in Oriya. She teaches in the Oriya Women's College in Rourkela. Her work has appeared in various magazines since 1977.

Kamala Das b. 1934, Punnayurkulam, Malabar. Daughter of Malayali poet, Balamani Amma, currently lives in Trivandrum; writes in both Malayalam (as Madhavi Kutty) and English; one of India's most well-known poets. Winner of many awards including the PEN award in 1963; in addition to over a dozen books in Malayalam, she has four collections of poetry in English.

Yashodhara Das b. 1949, Cuttack. She is a woman activist and trade unionist and writes about problems of the lower middle class and of women. At present she is busy with her new novel *Distant Dreams*.

Mamata Dash b. 1947, Jagatsinghpur, Cuttack, Orissa. She has to her credit three collections of poetry and one of short stories. A fourth collection is to be published shortly. She has been given a fellowship by the Cultural Department of India for her research work on the 'Radha Consciousness' in Indian Literature. Many of her poems have been translated into different Indian languages and into English. She was awarded the State Sahitya Akademi award for poetry in 1987.

Tilottama Sirkar Daswani b. 1934, Maharashtra. She holds a Ph.D. from Cornell University in Linguistics. A poet herself, her work in English has appeared in various Commonwealth publications in UK, USA, India and Canada. She lives in Delhi where she works for the Department of Adult Education (MHRD) as a consultant. She is the former Head of Department of English, JNU.

Jyotirmoy Datta b. 1936, Murshidabad. Grew up in rural South India. Journalist with the *Statesman*, 1956-68, lecturer at the University of Chicago; fellow, Iowa International Writers Program. Free-lance journalist, translator, editor of *Kolkata*. In English, his poems have appeared in *Triquarterly*, *Hudson Review* and in the *Penguin Book of Indian Writing*.

In Their Own Voice

Gauri Deshpande b. 1942, Maharashtra. She has three books of poems (in English), ten novels (in Marathi), sixteen volumes of the *Arabian Nights* (translated from English into Marathi), and three collections of poems in English to her credit. She holds a Ph.D. in English Literature and has had numerous articles, translations, and columns in books, periodicals and newspapers in India and abroad.

Eunice de Souza b. 1940. Ph.D. in English, University of Bombay; MA from Marquette University; currently the head of the Department of English at St. Xavier's College, Bombay. She has published three volumes of poetry: *Fix* (1979), *Women In Dutch Painting* (1988), and *Ways of Belonging* (1990); she is one of India's best-known poets writing in English.

Nabaneeta Dev Sen b. 1938, Calcutta. Named by Rabindranath Tagore, her parents were well-known writers. Essayist, poet, journalist; educated at Presidency College, at Cambridge and Harvard Universities. Ph.D. in Comparative Literature, Indiana University. She has to her credit three collections of poetry, six novels, four collections of short stories, four travelogues, and two volumes of literary criticism, one collection of *belles-lettres*, one collection of translated poems and two novels for childern. At present she is a professor of Comparative Literature at Jadavpur University, Calcutta.

Imtiaz Dharker b. 1954, Lahore. An MA in English and Philosophy from Glasgow University, now lives in Bombay. A former poetry editor of *Debonair*. Artist, and poet, her recent collection of poetry, *Purdah*, was published by Oxford University Press.

Vinay Dharwadker b. 1954, Pune. Brought up in New Delhi. Ph.D. on modern Indian poetry from the University of Chicago. He has taught at the University of Georgia at Athens, and is at present at the University of Oklahoma, Norman.

Aruna Dhere b. 1957, Pune. She started writing when she was ten years old and has two collections of poetry o her credit. One of the serious writers of Marathi poetry.

Ashwini Dhongde b. 1947, Pune. A lecturer in English at SNDT College, Pune. Her publications include four novels, one short story collection and a collection of poems, *Stree-sukta*.

Saroop Dhruv b. 1948, Gujarat. Active in the women's movement and other causes in Gujarat; her poetry spans the gamut from the highly intellectual to the popular women's *garbo*. The lyrics of one of her *garbo*, translated here by Sujata Bhatt, have gained wide reknown, and have been freely added to by the women of Gujarat, most of whom are not aware that the original lyrics are hers.

Chitra Banerjee Divakaruni b. 1956, Calcutta. Her poetry has appeared in *The Beloit Poetry Journal, Chelsea, Calyx, Colorado Review, Chicago Review, Primavera, Threepenny Review*, etc., reflecting her interest in women's issues and the immigrant experience. Three volumes of poetry, *Dark Like The River* (1987), *The Reason For Nasturtiums* (1990), and *Black Candle*, (1991) have been published. She had edited a collection of multicultural literature titled *Multitude*. She has received the Hackney Literary Award, 1988, Barbara Deming Memorial Award, 1989, a Santa Clara Arts Council and a Gerbode Award; she was nominated for the 1989, 1990 and 1992 Pushcart prize.

Charmayne d'Souza b. 1955, Bombay. A counsellor and family therapist, her first book of poems, *A Spelling Guide to Woman*, appeared in 1990. Her work has appeared in such diverse journals as *Illustrated Weekly of India, Kavi India, P.E.N.*, the *Sunday Observer, The Literary Endeavour*, the *Sahitya Akademi Journal*, and *ARC* (Canada).

Ketaki Kushari Dyson b. 1940, Calcutta. Educated in Calcutta and Oxford. Writing in many different genres and in both Bengali and English, she has several books to her credit. She resides in Oxford, UK.

Pia Ganguly b. 1959, Asansol. Educated at Presidency College and the University of California, Irvine. She embodies the cross-cultural pollination of ideas and visions. She lives and works in California.

Prabha Ganorkar b. 1945, Amravati, Maharashtra. She holds a Ph.D. and teaches Marathi literature at Elphinstone College, Bombay. She has two collections of poems published, *Vyateet* (1974), and *Vivarta* (1985).

Gagan Gill b. 1959, New Delhi, Published her first collection of poems in 1989. She was the youngest Indian writer to attend the International Writing Program at the University of Iowa in 1990. She was the literary editor of the Hindi *Sunday Observer* in New Delhi, where she resides with her writer-husband, Nirmal Verma.

Hiren Gohain b. 1939. He was educated in Calcutta, Delhi and Cambridge. He is the author of several volumes of literary and social criticism in Assamese. He was awarded the Sahitya Akademi award in 1989.

Padma Gole b. 1913, Tasgaon, Maharashtra. MA in Marathi, from SNDT University, Pune. A well-known poet in Marathi, with numerous volumes of poetry published. She was the State Award Winner for Poetry in 1963, 1972 and 1992; has also won recognition and awards for her children's literature and a one-act play.

Teji Grover b. 1955, Pathankot, Punjab. Her poems have appeared in all significant Hindi journals including *Poorvagrah, Sakshatkar* etc. Her first collection of poems was published in 1983 while the second collection and a novel will be published shortly. She received the Bharat Bhushan Agrawal award in 1989. At present she lives in Chandigarh where she teaches English.

Kamala Hemmige b. 1952, Hemmige, Mysore. Four collections of poetry, a short-story collection, and a novel to her credit. She works as a programme executive for Doordarshan in Bangalore.

Popati Hiranandani b. 1924, Hyderabad, Sind. One of seven children, she learned independence at a very early age. Educated at Benaras Hindu University. Deeply concerned with the recognition of Sindhi language and literature; has written novels, criticism, short stories, essays and an autobiography in addition to her poetry. A recipient of the Sahitya Akademi award, 1982.

B. Hrdayakumari b. 1930, Kerala. She was the principal of College for Women, Thiruvananthapuram, Kerala, and a professor of English. At present she lives in Thiruvananthapuram where she writes in English and Malayalam on educational and social topics.

Qurratulain Hyder born in Aligarh, she is a leading fiction writer of India writing in Urdu. She received the Sahitya Akademi award for a collection of short stories (1967). In 1990, she received India's most prestigious award for literature, the Jnanpith Award.

Ivara (V. Indra Bhavani) b. 1942, Aruppukkottai, Dt. Kamraj, Tamil Nadu. Also writes under the pen name of Indhu Varadan. An MA and M.Phil., in addition to her three collections of poems, *Mownappoovin Makaranthe Uccharippukkal*, *Nittham Eriyum Durgaigal*, and *Manniyunsa* (Transcreation), she also has a collection of short stories, *Nijangal* (Naked Truths) to her credit.

Sunita Jain b. 1941, Ambala. Received her MA and Ph.D. in the US. Author of about twenty-two books, she writes poetry and fiction in Hindi and English. She teaches English at IIT, Delhi.

Nayana Jani b. 1951, Katrasgarh, Bihar. MA, English. First poem published in 1976. She and her poet-husband reside in Ahmedabad, Gujarat, where they are exploring alternatives to formal education for their children.

A. Jaya Prabha b. 1957, Nagpur. MA, M.Phil. and Ph.D. in Telugu literature. The first 'feminist' writer in Telugu, she has published five volumes of poetry in addition to her two volumes of literary criticism. She has an anthology of love poems in Telugu forthcoming.

Bhagya Jayasudarshana b. 1948, Somwarpet, Dt. Kodagu, Karnataka. Her first collection, *Badukina Tekkeyalli*, was published in 1978. Two other collections of poetry, *Sullinacheya Satya* (1981) and *Kaleduhogiddane Manushya* (1990). She lives in Bangalore with her husband and three daughters.

Mamta Kalia b. 1940, Mathura. Holds an MA in English from Delhi University. Taught in colleges in Delhi and Bombay. At present she is principal of a college in Allahabad. Author of twenty books in Hindi, two books in English including poetry, short stories, novels and plays.

M. R. Kamala b. 1959, Metikurke, Karnataka. MA, and LL B she is at present a lecturer in Kannada. She has published two collections of poetry, *Shakuntopakhyana* and *Jane*, and an anthology of 102 poems by black women writers translated into Kannada, *Kattala Hoovina Hadu*.

Lakshmi Kannan b. 1947, Mysore. A bilingual writer in Tamil (pen name Kaaveri) and English, she lives and works in New Delhi. Nine volumes of poetry, fiction, criticism and translation; poetry abroad in *Encounter, Helix, New Letters*, etc.

Manju Kapur b. 1948, Amritsar. A lecturer in English at Miranda House, Delhi University. She has four children and is currently working on a novel.

Ketu Katrak b. 1952, Bombay. MA, University of Bombay; Ph.D. Bryn Mawr; currently teaches at the University of Massachusetts, Amherst. The author of *Wole Soyinka and Modern Tragedy*, her interests include post-colonial literature from Africa, India and the Caribbean.

Katyayani b. 1959, Gorakhpur in Eastern Uttar Pradesh Her poetry and stories have appeared in journals such as *Hansa, Vartaman Sahitya, Dinman, the Sunday Mail, Chauthi Duniya, Jansatta, Nai Rachna*, etc. Some of her poems, translated into English, have appeared in *Manushi*. A journalist, she has been active in the women's movement.

Ashok R. Kelkar b. 1929, Pune. Internationally known linguist, literary critic and translator. Has published widely in Marathi, English and Hindi on language, literature, the arts and related philosophical issues. He recently retired from Deccan College, Pune.

Arun Kolatkar b. 1932, Kohlapur. Graphic artist, painter, poet. Two collections of poetry, *Arun Kolatkarchya Kavita* (in Marathi), and *Jejuri* (in English). He was awarded the Commonwealth Poetry Prize in 1977.

Kamal Kumar b. 1942, Ambala, Hariyana. Reader at Jesus and Mary College, Delhi University. She has authored several books of fiction, poetry, and literary criticism: *Aparth*, *Pahchan*, *Bayan*, *Gawah*, etc. Writes articles on women and social issues. She comperes literary programmes and progammes on women, and participates in panel discussions on T.V. and All India Radio.

N. Krishna Kumari b. 1930, Guntur, Andhra Pradesh. She has an MA, and a Ph.D. in Telugu. Professor of Telugu, Osmania University. She has several publications to her credit amongst which are three collections of poetry. She received an award from the Andhra Pradesh Sahitya Akademi for best woman writer and the Suseela Narayana Reddy award, 1988.

Kusum (Kusum Karnik) b. 1934, Bombay. An MA in Psychology, she has taught, worked as a counsellor and works as a activist for social justice, social transformation, and reconstruction, ecological living. Concerned with women, children, tribals, and development.

Apabrita Lahiri b. 1965, Calcutta. She is the youngest of the poets from Bengal, she nevertheless has two volumes to her credit, *Haran Moni* (The Lost Gem) (1985) and *Shnatijal* (The Ablution) (1987). She resides in Calcutta.

Chitra Lahiri b. 1955, Calcutta. BA, Calcutta University. She is both a poet and a critic. In addition to her poetry, she plays the sitar, is a stage actress and an artist.

Jyoti Baburae Lanjewar b. 1950, Nagpur. An MA in Marathi, she holds an M.Phil. and Ph.D. as well. A prominent Dalit woman poet, she has one collection of poems, *Deesha*, as well as three other books to her credit. A new collection of poems is in the press.

Joyshri Lobo b. 1944, Lahore. Of Bengali and Punjabi background, married to a Goan planter; resides on a tea estate in Jalpaiguri, West Bengal. Her collection of poems, *Bittersweet*, and a collection of short stories, *The Untouchable's Wife*, were brought out by the Writers Workshop, Calcutta.

Pravasini Mahakud b. 1957, Koksara, Kalahandi, Orissa. An MA in Oriya, one of Orissa's most promising young poets, she has had hundreds of poems published in Oriya magazines. In addition to *Suparna*, her newly published novel, a collection of her poetry is slated for publication.

Anuradha Mahapatra b. 1957, Nandigram, Samasabad, Midnapur. MA, Bengali, Calcutta University. Three collections, *Chhaiphulstup*, *Adhibas Manikarnika*, and *Am Mukuler Gandha* have been published. In a community of writers drawn largely from the middle and upper classes, she is one of the few with a rural middle-class background. She works with marginalized, rural-based poor communities in Calcutta.

Jayanta Mahapatra b. 1928, Cuttack. Poet in English; also does translations from Oriya. Edited *Chandrabhaga*, a journal of new writing (1979-1986); edits *Kavyabharati*. Attended an International Writing Program at Iowa (1975).

Uma Maheswari b. 1967, Bodinayakanur. A 'housewife', her poems have appeared in *Kalki*; she writes regularly for *Kaanaiyazhi*. At present she lives in Andipatty, Madurai, Tamil Nadu.

Anna Sujatha Mathai b. 1934, Nagpur, into an old Syrian Christian family of Kerala. Has published three collections of poetry in English: *Crucifixions*, *We the Unreconciled*, and *The Attic of Night* (Rupa, 1991). Her poems have been published in anthologies and journals including *Chelsea* (NY), *2PLUS2* (Switzerland). Many of her poems have been translated into European and Indian languages. She lives in New Delhi where she writes short stories and critical reviews for several Indian journals and papers.

Shakunt Mathur b. 1920, Delhi. From a three-century-old metropolitan family tradition, she is the primary poet of the New Poetry Movement. She has three collections of poetry, *Chandni Chunar* (1960), *Abhi Aur Kuch* (1968), and *Lahar Nahin Tutegi* (1990).

R. Meenakshi b. 1947, Virudhunagar, Tamil Nadu. Poet, teacher, social worker; since 1976 she has been an educational researcher in Auroville (the international township founded by the Mother of Sri Aurobindo Ashram). She has four collections of poetry to her credit.

In Their Own Voice

Jaya Mehta b. 1932, Koliak, Dt. Bhavnagar, Gujarat. A leading poet in Gujarati with numerous volumes of poetry to her credit, she is head of the Department of Gujarati, SNDT College, Bombay.

Memchoubi is the pen-name of Arambam Ongbi Ibemhal b. 1955, Kwakeithel, Imphal, Manipur. She holds an MA in Manipuri, is editor of *Machaleima*, a women's quarterly. She has two collections of poems to her credit, *Nonggoubi* (1984) and *Androgi Mei* (1990).

Jyotsna Milan b. 1941, Bombay. She obtained MAs in Gujarati Literature as well as in English Literature and at present is the editor of *Anasuya*, a women's journal of SEWA published from Bhopal. Her publications include two novels: *Apne Saath* (1976) and *A Astu Ka* (1990); two collections of short stories: *Cheekh Ke Aar Paar* and *Khandahar, and Other Stories* (1982); and a collection of poems: *Ghar Nahin* (1989).

Sanghamitra Mishra b. 1953, Khandasahi, Cuttack, Orissa. D.Litt. in Oriya drama, her field of research is modern experimental drama and dramaturgy. She is a Reader in Oriya Literature at Utkal University, Bhubaneshwar; she has published five volumes of literary criticism in addition to her two collections of poetry.

Sucheta Mishra b. 1965, Berhampur, Orissa. Completed her postgraduate degree, and is at present teaching at Blessed Sacrament High School in Puri. Her poetry has appeared in leading journals in Orissa and in the *Telegraph*, and has been published in an anthology entitled *Purvaraga*.

Yashodara Mishra b. 1951, Orissa. She has to her credit three collections of short stories and a novel in Oriya and one collection of short stories in Hindi translation. A teacher of English Literature, her Ph.D. thesis was on Steinbeck's novels. She has worked in the Encyclopaedia Division of the Sahitya Akademi, New Delhi.

Debarati Mitra b. 1946, Calcutta. Four volumes of poetry; *Andha Schoole Ghanta Baje* (A Bell Rings in the School for the Blind) (1971), *Amar Putul* (My Doll) (1974), *Jubaker Snan* (The

Young Man's Bath) (1978), *Bhutera O Khuki* (Ghost and the Little Girl) (1988).

Aparna Mohanty b. 1952, Garapur, Dt. Kendrapara, Orissa. Lecturer in Oriya literature at Tulasi Women's College, Kendrapara. She is a well-known poet and critic of Orissa. She received her Ph.D. from Utkal University, under the guidance of Pratibha Satpathy.

Brahmotri Mohanty b. 1934, Markandeswara Sahi, Puri. Recipient of the Orissa Sahitya Akademi Award, 1983, and the Visuba Award of Prajatantra Pradchar Samiti, in 1962, 1976, and 1984. Has been publishing poetry for thirty-five years. Her first collection, *Avatarana*, appeared in 1972.

Giribala Mohanty b. 1947, Nampo, Balasore, Orissa. MA, Ph.D. from Visva Bharati Santiniketan. At present a Reader at F.M. College, Balasore. She has been writing poetry for three decades, with three collections to her credit.

Nirmala Mohanty b. 1948, Village Podaruan, Cuttack. She has published two poetry collections: *Anaeka Nidagha Pare*, and *Niraba Niryas*; a collection of short stories, *Aalapa*; two volumes of children's literature. She has been writing since 1965, has written for many journals and All India Radio, and has appeared on TV in Orissa.

Sasmita Mohanty b. 1967, Bhubaneswar. She has been writing poetry since 1984. She also writes short stories and children's literature. Her articles have appeared in various Oriya literary magazines and newspapers, and have been broadcast by All India Radio. She is the daughter of Nirmala Mohanty, a contemporary Oriya poetess.

Kanchankuntala Mukherjee b. 1953, Calcutta. A Ph.D. in Modern Bengali Poetry, at present she is a senior lecturer in Bengali. She has had four books of poetry and a translation from Sanskrit to Bengali of the *Gita Govinda* published. She has written poetry and essays for a variety of magazines.

Vijaya Mukhopadhyay b. 1937, Vikrampur, (now in Bangladesh). She holds an MA in Sanskrit. She edits, translates, teaches and has authored seven books of poetry. Actively involved in the Bengali poetry movement since 1964.

H. S. Mukthayakka b. 1954, Koppal, Dt. Raichur, Karnataka. She holds an MA and is at present a lecturer. Her publications include *Nanu Matthu Avanu*, a collection of poems, and two biographies, *Dhakkaya Bommanna* and *Shivasharne Mukthayakka*.

Asha Mundlay b. 1936, Pune. Anthropologist, linguist, and freelance writer, she teaches Marathi to foreign students. Has done field work on the language of the central Indian tribe, the Nihals. Interested in Women's Movements, published *Ghar*, a collection of essays on family disharmony.

Vrinda Nabar b. 1948, Bombay. A well-known writer, translator, media-personality and critic, she lectures at the University of Bombay and was the fiction editor for the *Independent* (India).

B. T. Lalita Naik b. 1945, Thangalitanda, Chikamangulur, Karnataka. Now living in Raichur, she is a member of the legislative council. Has published novels, short stories, as well as poetry.

Panna Naik b. 1933, Bombay. Emigree to US in 1960. Began writing poetry in 1972. MA, University of Pennsylvania. Five collections of poetry in Gujarati. Her poems appeared in English translation in *Massachusetts Review*, *Chandrabhaga*, and *Journal of South Asian Literature*. Her new collection, *Avanjavan*, is in press.

Pratibha Nandakumar b. 1955, Bangalore, Karnataka. MA, M. Phil. in Kannada. Considered one of the prominent young poets of Kannada; her third collection of poems, *Rastheyanchina Gaadi*, (1991) received the prestigious Muddana Kavya award.

Velcharu Narayana Rao (Nara) b. 1932, Ambakhandi, Andhra Pradesh. A literary critic and translator from Telugu, he teaches in the Department of South Asian Studies, University of Wisconsin, Madison. He was a Guggenheim Fellow in 1991-92.

Tejaswini Niranjana b. 1958, Dharwad, Karnataka. Has published two collections of poems—*Liquid Sapphire* (1974) and *Burnt Smoke and Wood Ash* (1978). Her poems have appeared in various journals in India and abroad.

Kondepudi Nirmala b. 1959, Hyderabad, Andhra Pradesh. Educated at Maris Stella College, Vijayawada. Her poems have been broadcast by All India Radio, and appeared in Telegu newspapers and magazines. She is the recipient of numerous state-level awards for her works on poetry.

Jameela Nishat b. 1955, Hyderabad, Andhra Pradesh. B.Sc., MA (English), Diploma (Theatre Arts). She has been writing since the age of twelve. Her work has been published in *Kitabnuma*, *Shair*, *Sabras*. She has read her poetry on Doordarshan, All India Radio and at many *mushairas*.

Mrinal Pande b. 1946, Tikamgarh. Well-known playwright and fiction writer in Hindi, with five collections of short stories, two novels and four plays to her credit, she is also a prominent media personality. The Editor of *Vama*, a *Times of India* Hindi monthly for women (1981-1985), and *Saptahik Hindustan* (weekly) of the *Hindustan Times*, she is the current joint editor of the *Hindustan Times* Hindi daily, *Hindustan*.

K. Ayyappa Paniker b. 1930, Kerala. Ph.D., Indiana University. Poet and critic in Malayalam, won the Kerala Sahitya Akademi Award with his first collection of poems. He has five volumes of poetry, two of criticism to his credit. Chief Editor, *Medieval Indian Literature*, Sahitya Akademi. Formerly, Head of the Institute of English, University of Kerala in Trivandrum.

K. Paramasivam 1933–1992, b. Viravanallur, Tirunelveli. A linguist, he lived in Madurai where he was director of the Tamil Language Center, American Institute of Indian Studies, and for thirty years taught at the American College. He translated over twenty English classics into Tamil. Ph.D., University of Chicago.

Uma Parameswaran born in Madras; grew up in Nagpur and Jabalpur. Recipient of the Smith-Mundt Fulbright fellowship to study English literature in the US; Ph.D. Michigan State University. Teaches Commonwealth Literature at University of Winnipeg. Three non-fiction books, including *The Perforated Sheet: Essays On Salman Rushdie's Art* have been published.

Geeta Parikh b. 1929, Bhavanagar. One of the most prominent women poets in Gujarati, an MA in Philosophy and Ph.D. in Literature of Gujarati women poets, she has five books of poetry to her credit and criticism and translations, and is a teacher of classical music.

Rajani Parulekar b. 1945, Pavas, Ratnagiri, Maharashtra. MA, Elphinstone College. Lecturer in Marathi, Burhani College. Maharashtra award for her collection of long, narrative poems, *Dirgha Kavita* (1985). Her latest collection, *Kahi Dirgha Kavita* was published in 1993.

Bharat Pathak b. 1935, Ahmedabad, Gujarat. A teacher of Social Work, he has translated Jayant Narlikar's science fiction from Marathi to Gujarati. He also writes poetry.

Anuradha Patil b. 1953, Pahur, Dt. Jalgaon, Maharashtra. She has three collections of poems, *Digant*, *Tarihee* and *Diwasendiwas* to her credit; the first two have won awards from the state of Maharashtra and from literary associations.

Hema Pattanshetti b. 1954, Dharwad. MA, Psychology, and MA, M.Phil., Kannada; lecturer in both Psychology and Kannada. A producer for All India Radio, has directed and written plays for the stage, the radio and the television, award-winning collections of poetry, a collection of short stories, seven other works.

Anuradha Potdar b. 1927, Ahmednagar, near Pune. Writing since the age of eleven, she has three collections of poetry and some critical work to her credit. A retired professor, and Head of the Department of Marathi, at a Pune college.

Amrita Pritam b. 1919. Her prodigious literary output includes sixteen volumes of poems, seventeen novels and four volumes of short stories. She was awarded the Sahitya Akademi award in 1956. Since 1966 she has been editing and publishing *Nagmani* (The Serpent's Jewel), a literary journal. In 1966, *Mahfil* (The Journal of South Asian Literature) brought out an issue devoted to her work, (vol. V, no. 3). A former member of the Rajya Sabha, she lives in New Delhi.

Savitri Rajeevan b. 1955, Kerala. Has been published in many anthologies such as *Puthukavithakal* and *Tiranjetutha 51 Kavithakal*, a regular contributor to Malayalam periodicals. Works with Samskar Keralam (a literary journal). Lives in Trivandrum.

Rajlukshmee Debee Bhattacharya b. 1927, Mymensingh (Bangladesh). BA, MA, (Calcutta University) Ph.D., (Pune University), was the Head of the Department of Philosophy at N. Wadia College, Pune, till 1987. In 1977, she lectured on Tagore's philosophy at Bryn Mawr and Harverford College, Philadelphia, U.S.A. In 1991, she attended the International Conference of Writers at Perth, Australia. In 1992, she visited England as a guest of the British Council, after her poem, *Punarnava* was awarded the first prize in a competition sponsored by the British Council. She has four published volumes of poetry and a volume of poems in English translation, *The Owl and Other Poems*, two novels and several short stories published in Bengali and English journals to her credit.

Nita Pramod Ramaiya b. 1941, Morvi, Gujarat. Teaches in the Post-Graduate Department of English at SNDT Women's University, Bombay. Seeking to invent a new 'women's' language in poetry.

Anuradha Ramanan b. 1947, Madras. Primarily, a well-known short-story writer in Tamil. She considers herself to be a 'twenty-second century' poet. Refuses to be bound by traditions. 'However man may write, there are things which men don't know; things only women see.'

A. K. Ramanujan b. 1929, Mysore. Poet and translator, with degrees in English and in Linguistics; a Fulbright scholar at Indiana University. Teaches in the Department of South Asian Languages and Civilizations and the Committee on Social Thought, University of Chicago. Recipient of the prestigious MacArthur award, he enjoys a well-deserved international reputation.

Chekuri Ramarao b. 1934, Illindalapadu, Dt. Khammam, Andhra Pradesh. Literary critic, and linguist, he holds a Ph. D. in Linguistics from Cornell University. He has taught at the

University of Delhi and was Dean, School of Language Development, Telugu University, Hyderabad. He is, at present, Professor and Dean of Humanities in Osmania University, Hyderabad.

V. V. B. Rama Rao b. 1938, Vizianagaram. ELT specialist, novelist, short story and feature writer, journalist, translator; six novels in Telugu, two in English have been published, as well as one on literary criticism, *Graham Greene's Comic Vision*.

C. Vimala Rao b. 1934. Educated at Mysore, the University of Pennsylvania, and the University of Wisconsin. She has two collections of poems (Writers Workshop, Calcutta) to her credit. Short stories published in journals in India and abroad. At present she is Professor of English, Lucknow University.

Pratima Ray b. 1942, Calcutta. She has had seven volumes of poetry published. Writing regularly for many periodicals, she attended the All India Poetry Festival at Bharat Bhavan in Bhopal in 1987.

Sunil B. Ray b. 1916, Dacca (now in Bangladesh). Since retiring from the IAS, has translated extensively from French, Spanish, Urdu and Persian to Bengali; and from Bengali to German, Persian, French and English. Amongst a wide range of publications is an English verse translation of the *Rubaiyat* of Omar Khayyam, and selected poems and short stories by German writers in Bengali translation.

Revathi Devi ca. 1951-1981, b. Guntur, Andhra Pradesh. She lived in various parts of India during her life. She pursued doctoral studies on Jean-Paul Sartre, although she did not complete her thesis. Her collection of poetry, *Silalolitha* (Stone-Tossed) appeared posthumously in 1981.

Anuradha Marwah Roy b. 1962, Ajmer, Rajasthan. Teaches in a Delhi University College. Besides poetry, also writes short stories, book reviews and articles. She has written a novel entitled *The Higher Education of Geetika Mehendiratta*, to be published shortly.

Padma Sachdev b. 1940, Jammu. Five published anthologies in Dogri; two prose works in Hindi. Recipient of the Sahitya

In Their Own Voice

Akademi Award (1971), and various other State and Union awards and honours. Here representing Dogri, she is a poet who is passionate, witty, as well as frequently irreverent.

Sulekha Samantaray b. 1954, Baripada, Orissa. Teaches English literature at SVM College, Jagatsinghpur. Has published one collection of poems in English. Her short stories and poems both in English and Oriya have appeared in many journals.

Sandhya S. b. 1961, Tumkur, Karnataka. MA, English, Bangalore University. Working for her Ph.D. on a comparative study of the historical plays of Shakespeare and Samsa. She has published translations in Kannada and English, including poetry of medieval Kannada women poets. She is also a Kannada playwright and director.

Malavika Rajbans Sanghvi b. 1958, Delhi. She is a freelance journalist who says her first love will always be poetry. A columnist for *Sunday Mid-day*, she has been India Editor for Harper's and Queen (UK) Since 1986.

Indira Sant b. 1914, Maharashtra. She has published seven volumes of poetry, as well as fiction for children and adults. In the 1940s she emerged as the most intensely lyrical of the *nava kavya* poets; in the past thirty years she has become an outspoken voice of middle-class women in contemporary Maharashtrian society.

Sarvamangala b. 1948, Dt. Shimoga, Karnataka. Has published many critical essays and poems in literary journals and one collection of poems, *Ammana Gudda*. Recipient of the State Sahitya Akademi Award. Teaches Kannada literature in Mysore.

Yashodhara Sathe b. 1951, Pune. MA, Marathi. Her collection of poems, *Tanamanchi Gani*, won the Maharashtra State Award. She also writes short stories and criticism. She is the daughter of the poet, Anuradha Potdar.

Pratibha Satpathy b. 1945, Cuttack, Orissa. She teaches at R.D. Women's College, Bhubaneshwar. She edits the literary quarterly, *Istahar*. She has seven volumes of poems, a book on Romanticism in modern Oriya poetry, and translations of works by Isaac Bashevis Singer and Pearl Buck to her credit. She received the Orissa Sahitya Akademi Award for poetry in 1986, and the prestigious Sarala Award of the state 1992.

Savithri ca. 1949-1991, b. Undeswarapuram, Andhra Pradesh. During her lifetime she fought against the male chauvinistic society relentlessly writing a number of articles, stories, poems, etc., ignoring her chronic illness due to tuberculosis. After her death, some friends brought out a comprehensive anthology of her literary works entitled *Savitri* under the editorship of Arangyakrishna.

Martha Ann Selby b. 1954, Nevada, Iowa. A Fulbright scholar, she is a Ph.D. candidate in South Asian Languages and Civilizations, University of Chicago. In 1981-82, she participated in the Iowa Poetry Workshop.

Nilima Sen-Gangopadhyay b. 1929, Calcutta. Teaches at Modern High School for Girls, Calcutta. Her poetry has appeared in magazines, newspapers, and on both Air India Radio and Doordarshan, Calcutta. A painter and pianist, she writes short stories and essays as well as poetry.

Mallika Sengupta b. 1960, Calcutta. She spent her childhood in places such as Burdwan, Birbhum and Krishnanagar District. Has published three collections of poems, *Challish Chander Ayu* (Lifespan of Forty Moons) (1984), *Ami Sindhur Meye* (Daughter of the Indus) (1989), and *Haghare O Debdasi* (The Destitute and The Temple Dancer) (1991).

Rajee Seth b. 1935, Nowshehra, NWFP (now Pakistan). MA, English Literature. She writes fiction, poetry, literary criticism, and articles. She is the co-editor of the literary Hindi journal *Yugasakshi*. She has four collections of short stories and a novel to her credit. A collection of poems is to be published shortly.

Shakuntala Devi b. 1945, Keonjhar, Orissa. In addition to a novel, *Arambharu Upasanghar*, and a collection of short stories, she has five collections of poetry to her credit. She was awarded the Orissa Sahitya Akademi award for her collection *Ananta Shayan* for the year 1989.

Rita Shahani b. 1934, Hyderabad, Sindh (Pakistan). She has four poetry collections, two novels, two short story collections, a travelogue, and a biography to her credit. Her poems, articles, stories and literary criticism appear regularly in magazines.

Arabinda Nath Sarma b. 1938, Sibsagar, Assam. MA (English), MA (History); has published two books, four books translated and about a hundred articles in English and Assamese on literary and historical topics published in leading journals and newspapers of Delhi, Assam and Bombay. His novel *Bandi* was exhibited in India Festival as a representative Assamese novel.

Ramachandra Sharma b. 1925, Karnataka. Educated in Bombay, Bangalore and London. Ph.D. in Psychology, University of London. He has lived and worked in India, Ethiopia, England and Zambia. He was involved with part of the Modern Poetry Movement in Karnataka during the 1950s. His collection, *Gestures,* was published in 1978. He is a poet and a short story writer.

Shafiq Fatima Sheira b. 1930, Nagpur. Received her MA from Nagpur University; currently lives in Hyderabad. A well-respected Urdu poet, she has published two volumes of her poetry, *Afaqe-e-Nawa*, and *Galla-e-Safoora*. Recipient of the Thirumalamba National Award in 1988.

Shanta Shelke b. 1922, Indapor, Pune. A professor as well as a writer, she has tried her hand at many literary forms, but her first love is poetry. She has been writing poetry for the last forty-five years and has written songs, poems for children and has translated poetry from other languages into Marathi.

Shree Devi b. 1948, Shillong, Assam. A member of a Rajput princely family, she has published two books with the Writers Workshop, Calcutta. Married, with one son, she lives in Delhi.

Beheroze Shroff b. 1951, Bombay. A student of Eunice de Souza, is influenced by her. 'Betwixt and between two worlds'; when not a poet, makes a living as a film-maker in India; M.F.A., Film and TV at UCLA and a master's degree in English at the University of Bombay. Her poems have been published in *P.E.N.*

(India), *Gray-Book*, *Massachusetts Review*, and *Making Waves: An Anthology of Asian Writing* (Boston).

Melanie Silgardo b. 1956, Bombay. Co-founder of Newground, a poet's co-operative publishing house. Her poems have been published in *Three Poets* (Newground, 1978) and in a single volume, *Skies of Design* (1985). She works as an editor at Virago Press, London.

L. Joychandra Singh b. 1949, Imphal, Manipur. He is the Secretary of the Manipur State Kala Akademi. He has translated T. S. Eliot's *The Wasteland* into Manipuri (1990).

Ila Rani Singh b. 1945, Shahmoura, Saharasa, Bihar. She has been writing in Maithili and Hindi since 1960. Has published four anthologies of poems, three books of literary criticism and translated six books into Maithili, Bengali and Hindi; her poems have appeared in *Mithila Darshan*, *Mithila Mihir*, *Maithili Kavita*, *Aakhar*, etc.

Anjani K. Sinha b. 1935, Bihar. Linguist and translator from Maithili and Hindi. Ph.D. University of Chicago, Member and formerly head of the Department of Linguistics at Delhi University, he is at present Provost of the International Students House, Delhi University.

Kabita Sinha b. 1931, Calcutta. Began publishing her writings in the early 1950s; has published a dozen novels since, a collection of short stories, and a number of volumes of poetry, including *Harina Boiri* (The deer that hates herself). A winner of the Lila and Motilal Prizes, she was at the International Writing Program at the University of Iowa in 1981-82.

Syed Sirajuddin b. 1925, Hyderabad. MA (English), Professor (Retd.) of English literature, Osmania University. Knows Urdu, English, Persian, Italian, some French and German. Poet, critic, and translator, his areas of interest are History, Philosophy and Art.

Aruna Sitesh b. 1945, Saharanpur, Uttar Pradesh. Reader, English, Indraprastha College. She has four volumes of short stories, two books of criticism on D. H. Lawrence to her credit, and is the co-editor of *Pratibha India*, co-translator of Bhartendu's *Andher Nageri Chaupat Raja* into English. She has edited *Glimpses: The Modern Indian Short Story* (1992) and *Beyond Gender and Geography American Women Writers: Modern Short Stories* (1993).

Sugathakumari b. 1934, Kerala. MA in Philosophy. Recipient of about twenty literary and social service awards, she has published fifteen books, most of them poetry. Actively involved in the Indian Nature Conservation Movement and service activities for mental patients and women in distress.

Sukrita (Sukrita Paul Kumar) b. 1949, Nairobi (Kenya). She teaches literature at Delhi University. She has published two collections of poems, *Oscillations* and *Apurna*. Her critical works are *Man, Woman and Androgyny*, *Conversations on Modernism*, and *The New Story*. She has also edited *Breakthrough*, a book of English translations of modern Hindi and Urdu short stories.

Thilakavathi b. 1952, Dharmapuri, Tamil Nadu. A senior officer in the IPS. 'To earn a livelihood I am a bureaucrat, but to live after death, I'm a poet. Women were bound by the family, treated like beasts of burden, not even allowed to learn the alphabet, but the lullabies and mourning songs have always been created by some (unknown) woman.' In addition to her collection of poems, she has authored six novels, eight novellas, and an autobiography.

Manjit Tiwana born in Punjab, she has published three collections of poems, a novel, and a full-length verse-play, *Paun Taragi* in Punjabi. She holds a Ph.D. in Psychology and teaches at G.C.G. Chandigarh.

Sunanda Tripathy b. 1964, Raghunathpur. She holds an MA and an LL B. She works as a lecturer of Sanskrit in Pipili College, Puri.

Sa. Usha b. 1954, Mysore. An MA in Literature, she teaches literature and edits the bi-monthly, *Samvada*. Two published collections, *Togalu Gombeya Atmakathe* (A Doll's Autobiography), for which she received the Udayonmukha Vardhamana Award (1986) and *Ee Nelada Hadu* (Song of the Earth) for which she received the Karnataka Rajya Sahitya Akademi Award (1990).

In Their Own Voice

Vaidehi (Janaki Srinivasamurthy) b. 1945, Kundapura, Dt. Dakshina Kannada, Karnataka. She has published four collections of short stories, a collection of poems, *Bindu Bindige*, a novel, *Asprushyaru*, and five children's plays.

Archana Verma b. 1946, Allahabad. She teaches Hindi at Miranda House, Delhi University. She has published two collections of poems and a collection of stories; is assistant editor of the literary journal, *Hans*.

Shefalika Verma b. 1943, Bhagalpur. Gold Medal for the best Maithili Prose Writing, she has three collections of short stories and sketches in addition to her poetry collections, *Vipralabdha*, *Anam Anubhuti*, *Rajani-Gandha* and *Thhahare Hue Pal*. Editor of *Chamakte Sitare* and *Tatka*, and is the head of the Department of Hindi, SNRK College, Saharsa, at present A. N. College, Patna.

Vimala b. 1960, Hyderabad. BA, 1980, Osmania University, Hyderabad. Actively involved in the Revolutionary writers movement, she edits *Vimochana*, a revolutionary organ of the CPI (ML-Janashakti). At present she is the General Secretary of 'Stree Vimukti' the Progressive Organization of Women (POW) in Andhra Pradesh.

Carolyne Wright b. 1949, Bellingham, Washington. Ph.D. creative writing/translation, Syracuse University. Poet (four published collections); translator from Spanish as well as Bengali. Her translations have appeared in *APR*, *Black Warrior*, *Triquarterly*, *Iowa Review*, *Nimrod* and *Seneca Review*. Began translating from Spanish after a 1971-72 Fulbright Study Grant to Chile, in Calcutta 1986-88 on an Indo-US Subcommission grant, and in Dhaka 1989-91, on a Fulbright.